Critters

of **Georgia**

Pocket Guide to Animals in Your State

ALEX TROUTMAN

produced in cooperation with
Wildlife Forever

PUBLICATIONS
Adventure
an imprint of AdventureKEEN

About Wildlife Forever

Wildlife Forever works to conserve America's outdoor heritage through conservation education, preservation of habitat, and scientific management of fish and wildlife. Wildlife Forever is a 501c3 nonprofit organization dedicated to restoring habitat and teaching the next generation about conservation. Become a member and learn more about innovative programs like the Art of Conservation®, The Fish and Songbird Art Contests®, Clean Drain Dry Initiative™, and Prairie City USA®. For more information, visit wildlifeforever.org.

Thank you to Ann McCarthy, the original creator of the Critters series, for her dedication to wildlife conservation and to environmental education. Ann dedicates her work to her daughters, Megan and Katharine Anderson.

Front cover photos by **karl umbriaco/shutterstock.com:** coyote, **Radiant Reptilia/shutterstock.com:** eastern indigo snake, **jadimages/shutterstock.com:** red-tailed hawk; Back cover photo by **lv-olga/Shutterstock.com:** double-crested cormorant

Edited by Brett Ortler and Jenna Barron
Cover and book design by Jonathan Norberg
Proofreader: Emily Beaumont

10 9 8 7 6 5 4 3 2 1

Critters of Georgia

First Edition 2000, Second Edition 2023

Published by Adventure Publications, an imprint of AdventureKEEN
310 Garfield Street South, Cambridge, Minnesota 55008
(800) 678-7006
www.adventurepublications.net

Cataloging-in-Publication data is available from the Library of Congress
ISBN 978-1-64755-411-8 (pbk.); 978-1-64755-412-5 (ebook)

Acknowledgments

I want to thank everyone who believed in and supported me over the years—a host of friends, family, and teachers. I want to especially thank my mom and my siblings Van, Bre, and TJ.

Dedication

I dedicate this book to my brother Van:
May you continue to enjoy the birds and wildlife in heaven.

This book is also dedicated to the South Cobb community, consisting of Mableton, Austell, and Powder Springs—one of the most loving and supportive communities I have been blessed to be a part of, with humble and hardworking people who are willing to lend a hand, offer a meal, or be a shoulder to lean on. I also extend much love to my M.A.P. community, as I wouldn't be the person I am today without y'all. May we continue to overcome barriers and showcase the South Cobb mentality to the world!

Next, this book is for all the kids who have a passion for nature and the outdoors, especially ones who identify as Black, Brown, Indigenous, and People of Color. May this be an encouragement to never give up, and if you have a dream and passion for something, pursue it relentlessly. I also hope to set an example that you can be successful as your full, authentic self!

Lastly, I dedicate this book to all those with ADHD and dyslexia, as well as all other members of the neurodivergent community. While our quirks make things more challenging, our goals are not impossible to reach; sometimes it takes a little more time and help, but we, too, can succeed!

Contents

About Wildlife Forever 2

Acknowledgments 3

Dedication 3

Introduction 6

Georgia: The Peach State 7

How to Use This Guide 9

Safety Note 9

Notes About Icons...............10

Mammals

American Beaver 12

Big Brown Bat....................14

Black Bear 16

Bobcat 18

Coyote 20

Eastern Chipmunk..............22

Eastern Cottontail...............24

Eastern Fox Squirrel............26

Gray Fox............................28

Long-tailed Weasel..............30

Manatee
(West Indian Manatee) 32

Mink.................................34

Northern Raccoon 36

Northern River Otter 38

Red Fox.............................40

Southeastern
Pocket Gopher 42

Southern Flying Squirrel 44

Spotted Skunk 46

Star-Nosed Mole 48

Tricolored Bat....................50

Virginia Opossum 52

White-tailed Deer 54

Birds

American Goldfinch............56

Anhinga 58

Bald Eagle 60

Barred Owl 62

Belted Kingfisher 64

Black Vulture/
Turkey Vulture...................66

Canada Goose....................68

Double-crested Cormorant .. 70

Eastern Towhee 72

Gray Catbird......................74

Great Blue Heron 76

Great Horned Owl.............. 78

Mallard 80

Northern Cardinal 82

Northern Mockingbird 84

Osprey 86

Painted Bunting................. 88

Peregrine Falcon................ 90

Red-tailed Hawk/
Red-shouldered Hawk 92

Roseate Spoonbill 94

Ruby-throated
Hummingbird 96

White Ibis 98

Wild Turkey 100

Wood Duck.......................102

Wood Stork.......................104

Reptiles and Amphibians

Alligator Snapping Turtle ...106

American Alligator 108

Copperhead......................110

Cottonmouth
(Water Moccasin)..............112

Diamondback Terrapin 114

Eastern Coral Snake...........116

Eastern Garter Snake 118

Eastern Glass Lizard 120

Eastern Indigo Snake 122

Eastern Kingsnake 124

Eastern Tiger
Salamander.......................126

Gopher Tortoise.................128

Green Anole 130

Loggerhead Sea Turtle/
Green Sea Turtle 132

Rattlesnakes.....................134

Snapping Turtle, Common ..136

Glossary...........................138

Checklist...........................140

The Art
of Conservation®................142

Photo Credits....................143

About the Author...............144

Introduction

My passion for nature started when I was young. I was always amazed by the sunlit fiery glow of the red-tailed hawks as they soared overhead when I went fishing with my family. The red-tailed hawk was my spark bird—the bird that captures your attention and gets you into birding. Through my many encounters with red-tailed hawks, and other species like garter snakes and coyotes, I found a passion for nature and the environment. Stumbling across conservationists like Steve Irwin, Jeff Corwin, and Jack Hanna introduced me to the field of Wildlife Biology as a career and gave birth to a dream that I was able to accomplish and live out: serving as a Fish and Wildlife Biologist for governmental agencies, as well as in the private sector.

My childhood dream was driven by a desire to learn more about the different types of ecosystems and the animals that call our wild places home. Books and field guides like this one whet my thirst for knowledge. Even before I could fully understand the words on the pages, I was drawn to books and flashcards that had animals on them. I could soon identify every animal I was shown and tell a fact about it. I hope that this edition of *Critters of Georgia* can be the fuel that sustains your passion for not only learning about wildlife, but also for caring for the environment and making sure that all are welcome in the outdoors. For others, may this book be the spark that ignites a flame for wildlife preservation and environmental stewardship. I hope that this book inspires children from lower socioeconomic and minority backgrounds to pursue their dreams to the fullest and be unapologetically themselves.

By profession, I'm a Fish and Wildlife Biologist, and I'm a nature enthusiast through and through. My love for nature includes making sure that everyone has an equal opportunity to enjoy the outdoors in their own way. So, as you use this book, I encourage you to be intentional in inviting others to appreciate nature with you. Enjoy your discoveries and stay curious!

–Alex Troutman

Georgia: The Peach State

Georgia is famous for its warm climate, rich history, and its many peach orchards. For more than 12,000 years, Georgia has been home to many different groups of Indigenous people, from the Paleoindian Period (12,000-8,000 years ago) to familiar groups such as the Cherokee, Muskogee, the Creek, Chickasaw, Choctaw, the Apalachee, and many others. The first Europeans to visit Georgia were Spanish conquistadors, including Hernando de Soto, who visited in 1540. The British claimed Georgia as a colony in 1732, making it one of the original thirteen colonies. It was named for the king at the time, King George II. After the Revolutionary War, Georgia became an American state, and the US government forcibly removed many of the Indigenous people on the "Trail of Tears," a forced march to reservations in Oklahoma without adequate food or clothing, leading to the death of thousands of people. Georgia was later the site of many important events in US history, from famous Civil War battles to the Civil Rights Movement, and today the state is well-known for high-tech industries, as a popular filming location, and, of course, for its agriculture.

Georgia has several different biomes, or large areas with different plant and animal communities. In the northwest is the Appalachian Plateau, which has the 2,392-foot-tall Lookout Mountain. The Blue Ridge Mountains are found in the northeast, with the highest point being 4,784 feet. The area also includes forests of poplar, oak, and hickory trees, many of which are covered in the creepy-yet-cool Spanish moss. The southern part of the state is home to the Atlantic Coastal Plain, with rivers, swamps, and the Atlantic Ocean. Georgia is home to part of the Okefenokee Swamp, one of the largest swamps in North America.

These many types of environments shelter a huge variety of animals and plants: the state is home to more than 80 different kinds of mammals, more than 400 bird species, and more than 170 species of reptiles and amphibians. This is your guide to the animals, birds, and reptiles and amphibians that call Georgia home.

Some of Georgia's most iconic plants, animals, and other natural resources are now officially recognized as state symbols. Get to know them below and see if you can spot them all! You'll probably encounter the state nickname and motto, so I've included them here too.

State Bird:
Brown
Thrasher

State Fruit:
Peach

State Tree:
Southern Live Oak

State Flower:
Cherokee Rose

State Fish:
Largemouth
Bass

State Butterfly:
Eastern Tiger
Swallowtail

State Reptile:
Gopher Tortoise

State Gemstone:
Quartz

**State
Nickname:**
The Peach
State

State Motto:
Wisdom,
Justice,
Moderation

How to Use This Guide

This book is your introduction to some of the wonderful critters found in Georgia; it includes 22 mammals, 28 birds, and 18 reptiles and amphibians. It includes some animals you probably already know, such as deer and bald eagles, but others you may not know about, such as eastern indigo snakes or anhingas. I've selected the species in this book because they are widespread (northern cardinal, page 82), abundant (white-tailed deer, page 54), or well-known but hard to spot (coyote, page 20).

The book is organized by types of animals: mammals, birds, and reptiles and amphibians. Within each section, the animals are in alphabetical order. If you'd like to look for a critter quickly, turn to the checklist (page 140), which you can also use to keep track of how many animals you've seen! For each species, you'll see a photo of the animal, along with neat facts and information on the animal's habitat, diet, its predators, how it raises its young, and more.

Safety Note

Nature can be unpredictable, so don't go outdoors alone, and always tell an adult when you're going outside. All wild animals should be treated with respect. If you see one—big or small—don't get close to it or attempt to touch or feed it. Instead, keep your distance and enjoy spotting it. If you can, snap some pictures with a camera or make a quick drawing using a sketchbook. If the animal is getting too close, is acting strangely, or seems sick or injured, tell an adult right away, as it might have rabies, a disease that can affect mammals. The good news is there's a rabies vaccine, so it's important to visit a doctor right away if you get bit or scratched by a wild animal.

Notes About Icons

Each species page includes basic information about an animal, from what it eats to how it survives the winter. The book also includes information that's neat to know; in the mammals section, each page includes a simple track illustration of the animal, with approximate track size included. And along the bottom, there is an example track pattern for the mammal, with the exception for those that primarily glide or fly (flying squirrels and bats).

On the left-hand page for each mammal, a rough-size illustration is included that shows how big the animal is when compared to a basketball.

Also on the left-hand page, there are icons that tell you when each animal is most active: nocturnal (at night), diurnal (during the day), or crepuscular (at dawn/dusk), so you know when to look. If an animal has a "zzz" icon, it hibernates during the winter. Some animals hibernate every winter, and their internal processes (breathing and heartbeat) slow down almost entirely. Other animals only partially hibernate, but this still helps them save energy and survive through the coldest part of the year.

nocturnal
(active at night)

diurnal
(active during day)

crepuscular
(most active at dawn and dusk)

hibernates/deep sleeper
(dormant during winter)

ground nest   cup nest   platform nest   cavity nest   migrates

On the left-hand side of each bird page, the nest for the species is shown, along with information on whether or not the bird migrates; on the right-hand side, there's information on where it goes.

Did you know?

Beavers are rodents! Yes, these flat-tailed mammals are rodents, like rats and squirrels. In fact, they are the largest native rodents in North America. Just like other rodents, beavers have large incisors, which they use to chew through trees to build dams and dens. Beavers are the original wetland engineers. By damming rivers and streams, beavers create ponds and wetlands.

Size Comparison   Most Active   Track Size

6"

American Beaver

Castor canadensis

Size: Body is 25–30 inches long; tail is 9–13 inches long; weighs 30–70 pounds

Habitat: Wooded wetland areas near ponds, streams, and lakes

Range: Beavers can be found throughout Georgia and in much of the rest of the United States.

Food: Leaves, twigs, and stems; they also feed on fruits and aquatic plant roots. Throughout the year they gather and store tree cuttings, which they eat in winter.

Den: A beaver's home is called a lodge. It consists of a pile of branches that is splattered with mud and vegetation. Lodges are constructed on the banks of lakes and streams and have exits and entrances that are underwater.

Young: Young beavers (kits) are born in late April through May and June in litters of 3–4. After two years they are considered mature and will be forced out of the den.

Predators: Bobcats, cougars, bears, wolves, and coyotes. Human trappers are major predators too.

Tracks: A beaver's front foot looks a lot like your hand; it has five fingers. The hind (back) foot is long, with five separate toes that have webbing or extra skin between them.

Beavers range from dark brown to reddish brown. They have a stocky body with hind legs that are longer than the front legs. The beaver's body is covered in dense fur, but its tail is naked and has special blood vessels that help it cool or warm its body.

Did you know?

It's a common misconception that bats are blind, but, in fact, they can see. However, they still rely on a special technique called echolocation to find food and to travel throughout the night sky. A female bat of reproductive age can eat her own body weight in insects in a single night. She does so while eating on the wing, meaning eating while in flight.

Size Comparison   Most Active   Hibernates

Big Brown Bat

Eptesicus fuscus

Size: 4–5 inches long; wingspan is 12–16 inches; weighs ½–1 ounce

Habitat: Cities, forests, deserts, mountains, and meadows

Range: Big brown bats are found statewide in Georgia year-round. They can also be found in north-central areas of Canada, throughout the US into Mexico, Central America, and northern areas of South America.

Food: Insectivorous (insect eater); beetles make up most of their diet. They also feed on flies, wasps, and moths.

Den: Roosts in a nursing colony that may contain 40–100 or more pregnant females. Reproductive males, or bachelors, usually roost alone or in small groups. Bats roost in mines, tree cavities, under bridges and other manmade structures, and in rock crevices.

Young: Young bats (pups) are born blind, without fur, between May and June. Pups will feed on milk for approximately 4–5 weeks. They will start the process of learning to fly around 3–5 weeks and become independent a couple of weeks later.

Predators: Snakes, owls, raccoons, feral cats, and humans

Tracks: Though they are rarely on the ground to leave a track, it would show as one thumbprint from the forearm and a hind footprint.

Big brown bats are large and have a furry back that's glossy brown to earthy red. They have a light-brown belly, hairless black wings, and rounded ears. In winter, they hibernate in tree cavities, manmade structures, and rock crevices. They maintain temperatures above 31 degrees and up to 42 degrees Fahrenheit.

The big brown bat does not often leave tracks.

Did you know?

Female bears weigh between 90 and 300 pounds and are smaller than the average adult human male in the US. But don't let their small size fool you; with a bite force around 800 pounds per square inch (PSI) and swiping force of over 400 pounds, these bears are not to be taken lightly.

Size Comparison   Most Active   Track Size 6–7"   Hibernates

Black Bear

Ursus americanus

Size: 5–6 feet long (nose to tail); weighs 90–600 pounds

Habitat: Forests, mountains, lowland areas, and swamps

Range: In Georgia, they can be found in three specific regions: near the Okefenokee Swamp in the south, the mountains in the north, and in central portions of the state. They are found in much of North America from northern Canada down into Mexico.

Food: Berries, fish, crops, small mammals, wild grapes, tree shoots, ants, bees, and even deer fawns

Den: Denning usually starts in December, with bears emerging in late March or April. Dens can be either dug (out of a hillside, for example) or constructed with materials such as leaves, grass, and moss.

Young: Two cubs are usually born at one time (a litter), often in January. Cubs are born without fur and blind, with pink skin. They weigh 8–16 ounces.

Predators: Humans and other bears. Sometimes, other carnivores, such as mountain lions, wolves, coyotes, or even bobcats, will prey on black bears. Cubs are especially vulnerable.

Tracks: Front print is usually 4–6 inches long and 3½–5 inches wide, with the hind foot being 6–7 inches long and 3½–5 inches wide. The feet have five toes.

Black bears are usually black in color, but they can be many different variations of black and brown. Some even have grayish, reddish, or blonde fur.

Did you know?

Bobcats get their name from their short tail; a "bob" is a type of short haircut. They have the largest range of all wild cats in the United States. Bobcats can even hunt prey much larger than themselves; in fact, they can take down prey that is over four times their size, such as white-tailed deer!

Size Comparison   Most Active   Track Size

Bobcat

Lynx rufus

Size: 27–48 inches head to tail; males weigh around 30 pounds, while females weigh 24 pounds or so

Habitat: Dense forests, scrub areas (forests of low trees and bushes), swamps, and even some urban (city) areas

Range: In Georgia, they have been reported in every county of the state; they are widespread throughout the United States.

Food: Squirrels, birds, rabbits and snowshoe hares, and white-tailed deer fawns; occasionally even adult deer and porcupines!

Den: Dense shrubs, caves, or even hollow trees; dens can be lined with leaves or moss.

Young: Bobcats usually breed in early winter through spring. Females give birth to a litter of 2–4 kittens. Bobcats become independent around 7–8 months, and they reach reproductive maturity at 1 year for females and at 2 years for males.

Predators: Occasionally fishers and coyotes; humans also hunt and trap bobcats for fur.

Tracks: Roughly 2 inches wide; both front and back paws have four toe pads and a carpal pad (a pad below the toe pads).

Bobcats have a white belly and a brown or pale-gray top with black spots. The tail usually has a black tip. They are mostly crepuscular (say it, cre-pus-cue-lar), which means they are most active in the dawn and twilight hours.

Did you know?

Coyotes are the biggest group of large predators in Georgia. At one time, coyotes were only found in the central and western parts of the US, but now with the help of humans (eliminating predators and clearing forests), they can be found throughout most of the country.

Size Comparison Most Active Track Size

2"

Coyote
Canis latrans

Size: 3–4 feet long; weighs 21–50 pounds

Habitat: Urban and suburban areas, woodlands, grasslands, and farm fields

Range: Coyotes are found throughout Georgia. They are also found throughout the US and Mexico, the northern parts of Central America, and southern Canada.

Food: A variety of prey, including rodents, birds, deer, and sometimes livestock

Den: Coyotes will dig their own dens but will often use old fox or badger dens, or hollow logs.

Young: 5–7 pups, independent around 8–10 months

Predators: Bears and wolves; humans trap and kill for pelts and to "protect" livestock.

Tracks: Four toes and a carpal pad (the single pad below the toe pads) can be seen on all four feet.

Coyotes have a brown, reddish-brown, or gray back fur with a lighter gray to white belly. They have a longer muzzle than other wild canines. They are active mostly during the night (nocturnal) but also during the twilight and dawn hours (crepuscular).

Did you know?
Chipmunks get their English name from the "chip" or alert calls they use when they sense a threat. Eastern chipmunks are not fully herbivores (plant eaters); in fact, they eat a variety of things, including other mammals and amphibians, like frogs.

Size Comparison   Most Active   Track Size   Hibernates

¾"

Eastern Chipmunk

Tamias striatus

Size: Body is 3–6 inches long; tail is 3–4 inches long; weighs 2½–5½ ounces

Habitat: Suburban areas, woodlands, and dense scrub areas

Range: Found throughout Georgia, the eastern US, and southern Canada

Food: Berries, nuts, seeds, frogs, insects

Den: Has multiple chambers (or rooms); the entrance is usually hidden under brush, fallen trees, rock piles, and human-made landscaping items.

Young: 2–8 young (kits) per litter, 2 litters per year. Born blind and without fur. Weigh under an ounce at birth. Eyes open at 4 weeks, and it becomes independent at 8 weeks.

Predators: Coyotes, feral and outdoor house cats, snakes, weasels, bobcats, hawks, and owls

Tracks: The front foot has four digit (toe) pads and is ½ inch long; the hind foot has five digit pads and is just under ¾ of an inch.

Chipmunks are small rodents with brown base colors, seven alternating stripes, and white bellies. During winter, they will stay underground. They hide food in underground caches that they will feed on through the winter.

Did you know?

The eastern cottontail gets its name from its short, puffy tail that looks like a cotton ball. A cottontail can travel up to 18 miles per hour! Rabbits have great hearing and eyesight. They can almost see all the way around them (360 degrees). On days with high wind, they will bed down in a burrow because the wind interferes with their ability to hear and detect predators.

Size Comparison   Most Active   Track Size

3½"

Eastern Cottontail
Sylvilagus floridanus

Size: 16–19 inches long; weighs 1½–4 pounds

Habitat: Forests, swamps, orchards, deserts, and farm areas

Range: Found throughout Georgia; through the eastern US to Arizona and New Mexico; isolated ranges in the Pacific Northwest

Food: Clovers; grasses; wild strawberries; garden plants; and twigs of a variety of trees, including maple, oak, and sumac

Den: Rabbits don't dig dens; they bed in shallow, grassy, saucer-shaped depressions (holes) or under shrubs. They will sometimes use woodchuck dens in the winter.

Young: They usually have 2–4 kits at one time, but it's not uncommon to have 7 or more. Born naked and blind, they weigh about an ounce (about the same weight as a slice of bread) and gain weight very quickly.

Predators: Owls, coyotes, eagles, weasels, humans, and foxes

Tracks: The front foot is an inch long with four toe pads; the hind foot is 3½ inches long.

An eastern cottontail sports thick brown fur with a white belly, a gray rump, and a white "cotton" tail. During the winter, it survives by eating bark off of fruit trees and shrubs.

Did you know?

The eastern fox squirrel's bones appear pink under ultraviolet (UV) light, a type of light human eyes can't see. Squirrels accidentally help plant trees by forgetting whey they previously buried nuts. Sometimes, they seem to pretend to bury nuts to throw off would-be nut thieves.

Size Comparison   Most Active   Track Size

2½"

Eastern Fox Squirrel

Sciurus niger

Size: 19–28 inches long; weighs 1–3 pounds

Habitat: Open woodlands, suburban areas, and dense forests

Range: They are found throughout Georgia and the eastern United States to Texas and as far north as the Dakotas.

Food: Acorns, seeds, nuts, insects such as moths and beetles, birds, eggs, and dead fish

Den: Ball-shaped dreys, or nests, are made of vegetation like leaves, sometimes in tree cavities.

Young: 2–3 kits are born between December and February and May and June. Kittens are born naked and weigh half an ounce; they are cared for by their parents for the first 7–8 weeks. They can reproduce by around 10–11 months for males and 8 months for females.

Predators: Humans, hawks, cats, coyotes, bobcats, and weasels

Tracks: The front tracks have four digits (toes), and the hind feet have five digits.

The eastern fox squirrel is the largest tree squirrel in Georgia. It is gray or reddish brown with a yellowish or light-brown underside. There is also a black and smoky-gray color phase. Both the male and female look the same.

Did you know?

Gray foxes are the only member of the dog family in the US that can climb trees well. They have semi-retractable claws, almost like cats, enabling them to hang onto trees.

Size Comparison   Most Active   Track Size

1½"

Gray Fox

Urocyon cinereoargenteus

Size: 2½–3½ feet long; weighs 6–10 pounds

Habitat: Forests, grasslands, urban (city) areas, and brushy and scrub-heavy areas near water sources

Range: Much of the continental United States; in Georgia, they can be found statewide.

Food: Omnivorous (eating both plants and animals, including birds, insects, mice, and rabbits). Also eats apples, nuts, grasses, various berries, and corn

Den: Usually only dens during mating seasons. Sometimes they use abandoned dens of other animals that they will widen or extend; also uses hollowed-out trees and cavities, caves, and crevices in rocky areas.

Young: Kits or pups, sometimes called cubs, are born in April or May; litters of 4–5 young are born at one time; young feed on milk for approximately 3 weeks and are then fed solids. At around 4 months they learn to hunt, and they eventually leave the family around the 10-month mark.

Predators: Bobcats, great horned owls, coyotes, and humans

Tracks: Front paw is 1¾–2 inches long and 1¾ inches wide. Hind foot is 1½ inches long and 1¼–1¾ inches wide.

Males are a bit larger than females. Fur comes in various mixtures of reds, grays, white, and black. The breast, belly, and side areas are a brownish red. The head is salt-and-pepper (mixture of gray, white, and black) with a white muzzle or nose area, cheeks, and throat. The tail has a distinctive black stripe that runs to the tip and bushes out.

Did you know?

Weasels are small but tough! They will attack prey over three times their own size, and they help control rodent and pest species by eating mice, voles, and other small mammals.

Size Comparison   Most Active   Track Size

1¾"

Long-tailed Weasel

Mustela frenata

Size: 14–18 inches long; weighs 5 ounces to 1 pound

Habitat: Forests, farms, and rocky areas

Range: Weasels can be found throughout Georgia and the rest of the United States, except for a small pocket in southern California, Nevada, and Arizona.

Food: Ducks and other birds, frogs, rodents, rabbits, and sometimes domesticated chickens and eggs; they will hide extra food to eat later.

Den: Weasels will dig dens but will also use rock piles, abandoned burrows of other animals, or hollow logs. Dens are covered with fur and grass.

Young: 4–8 kits are born in April; they reach adult weight within 4 months.

Predators: Hawks, owls, coyotes, foxes, humans, and cats

Tracks: The front foot is wider than the hind foot. Each foot has five toe pads with four claws extending from them.

Long-tailed weasels have several color phases, including alternating from brown to white as the seasons change from summer to winter.

Did you know?

Manatees are nicknamed *sea cows* because, like cows, they are slow-moving plant eaters. They eat seagrasses and other aquatic plants. Manatees graze for 6–8 hours a day and consume over 5% of their body weight in plant material. They have a special top lip that aids them in eating. Manatees use their lips to grab food, much like how an elephant uses it trunk.

Size Comparison   Most Active

Manatee (West Indian Manatee)

Trichechus manatus

Size: 9–14 feet or longer; weighs 400–1,200 pounds

Habitat: Coastal wetland areas such as marshes, mangroves (trees and shrubs growing on the coast), river areas, and inland areas associated with natural springs

Range: Manatees can be found along the southeastern US coast, as well as along the coasts of some Central and South American countries. In Georgia, they are found along the Atlantic coastline.

Food: Aquatic vegetation (plants found in water), like sea grass and eelgrass. Sometimes fish and invertebrates

Den: No den. Calves are born underwater, and the mom provides care.

Young: One calf is born at a time. Calves feed on milk for about 3 weeks and then transition to consuming plants. They depend on their mother for 2 years. Females reach reproductive maturity around 4 years but will usually breed at around 7–8 years. Males mature at around 9–10 years.

Predators: Due to their size and habitat, adult manatees do not have many natural predators other than humans (boat collisions, fishing gear entanglements, and pollution). Young can sometimes fall prey to alligators and some species of sharks.

Tracks: They leave no tracks because they are in the water.

Manatees are gray to brownish gray. They are sparsely covered with hair on their body. Their nose area is covered with thick whiskers that they use to locate food and sense their environment. They have flippers and a paddle- or spoon-shaped tail.

33

Did you know?

Mink have webbed feet, like otters. Although they usually dive and swim short distances, mink can dive over 13 feet deep and swim for over 95 feet underwater, if necessary!

Size Comparison   Most Active   Track Size

1¾"

Mink
Mustela vison

Size: 16–27 inches long; weighs 1½–3½ pounds

Habitat: Wetland areas with dense vegetation near streams, lakes, and swamps

Range: They are found across much of Georgia, as well as throughout most of the US and Canada.

Food: Fish, eggs, snakes, muskrats, farm animals, small mammals, and aquatic animals such as crawfish

Den: Their dens are near water, in holes in the ground, hollow logs, and old muskrat and beaver lodges; they will use grass or fur from prey as bedding.

Young: At birth, they weigh less than an ounce; mothers give birth to 3–6 young, called kits. They are mature at 1 year old.

Predators: Otters, birds of prey, wolves, coyotes, bobcats, internal parasites, and humans (who trap them for fur)

Tracks: Both the front and hind tracks resemble a gloved hand. Both the left and right tracks are seen parallel to each other because the mink often bound (leap) when moving. Tracks are usually seen near water.

A mostly nocturnal (active at night) animal, it has a shiny or glossy dark-brown coat that it keeps all year long. Mink usually have a white or pale-yellow chest patch or bib on the throat that sometimes extends to the belly.

Did you know?

The raccoon is great at catching fish and other aquatic animals, such as mussels and crawfish. They are also excellent swimmers but they apparently avoid swimming because the water makes their fur heavy. Raccoons can turn their feet 180 degrees; this helps them when climbing, especially when going head-first down trees.

Size Comparison   Most Active   Track Size   Hibernates

3"

Northern Raccoon

Procyon lotor

Size: 24–40 inches long; weighs 15–28 pounds

Habitat: Woody areas, grasslands, suburban and urban areas, wetlands, and marshes

Range: They are found throughout Georgia and the US; they are also found in Mexico and southern Canada.

Food: Eggs, insects, garbage, garden plants, berries, nuts, fish, carrion, small mammals, and aquatic invertebrates like crawfish and mussels

Den: Raccoon dens are built in hollow trees, abandoned burrows, caves, and human-made structures.

Young: 2–6 young (kits) are born around March through July. They are born weighing 2 ounces, are around 4 inches long, and are blind with lightly colored fur.

Predators: Coyotes, foxes, bobcats, humans, and even large birds of prey

Tracks: Their front tracks resemble human handprints. The back tracks sort of look like human footprints.

The northern raccoon has dense fur with variations of brown, black, and white streaks. It has black, mask-like markings on its face and a black-and-gray/brownish ringed tail. During the fall, it will grow a thick layer of fat to aid in staying warm through the winter.

Did you know?

Otters are good swimmers and can close their nostrils while diving. This allows them to dive for as long as 8 minutes and to depths of over 50 feet. Otter fur is the thickest of all mammal fur. River otters have an incredible 67,000 hairs for every square centimeter!

Size Comparison Most Active Track Size

3"

Northern River Otter

Lontra canadensis

Size: 29–48 inches long; weighs 10–33 pounds

Habitat: Lakes, marshes, rivers, and large streams; suburban areas

Range: Otters can be found throughout Georgia; they are found across much of the US, except parts of the Southwest and portions of the central US.

Food: Fish, frogs, snakes, crabs, crawfish, mussels, birds, eggs, turtles, and small mammals. They sometimes eat aquatic vegetation too.

Den: They den in burrows along the river, usually under rocks, riverbanks, hollow trees, and vegetation.

Young: 2–4 young (pups) are born between November and May. Pups are born with their eyes closed. They will leave the area at around 6 months old and reach full maturity at around 2 or 3 years.

Predators: Alligators, coyotes, bobcats, bears, and dogs

Tracks: Their feet have nonretractable claws and are webbed.

Northern river otters have thick, dark-brown fur and a long, slender body. Their fur is made up of two types: a short undercoat and a coarse top coat that repels water. They have webbed feet and a layer of fat that helps keep them warm in cold water.

Did you know?
The red fox is a great jumper and can leap over 13 feet in one
bound. Red foxes are also fast, as they can run up to 30 miles
per hour. Red foxes, like wild cats, will hide their food to eat
later, often under leaf litter or in holes.

Size Comparison   Most Active   Track Size

2¼"

Red Fox

Vulpes vulpes

Size: 37–42 inches long; weighs 8–15 pounds

Habitat: Grasslands, forest edges, farm fields, and suburban areas

Range: Foxes are common throughout Georgia; they can be found nearly in all of the US, except for the Southwest.

Food: Omnivores (they eat both meat and plants); they eat frogs, birds, snakes, small mammals, insects, seeds, nuts, and fruit.

Den: They dig underground dens, sometimes several at once, splitting a litter (babies) between the two. They also use old badger or groundhog holes or tree roots for den sites.

Young: 3–7 young (kits) are born; pups will nurse (drink milk from the mother) for around 10 weeks and will become independent at around 7 months.

Predators: Coyotes, lynx, cougars, and other species of carnivores. Humans trap and hunt foxes for fur.

Tracks: Their footprints resemble dog tracks and have four toe pads; they walk in a line with the hind foot behind the front.

The red fox is a medium-size predator with a burnt orange or rust-like red coat with a bushy, white-tipped tail. The legs are usually black or grayish. The red fox's tail is about one third of its body length.

Did you know?

The southeastern pocket gopher is a fossorial animal, meaning that it spends most of its life underground. They get their name "pocket gopher" from the external cheek pouches that they have. These pouches aid in carrying food to storage areas. Look for signs of gophers by locating tunnels just below the surface or volcano-shaped mounds at the surface.

Size Comparison   Most Active   Track Size

3/4"

42

Southeastern Pocket Gopher

Geomys pinetis

Size: 10–11½ inches long; weighs 4½–7½ ounces

Habitat: Dry, sandy, hilly habitats, grasslands, longleaf pine areas, urban (city) and suburban (neighborhood) areas, shrublands, farm fields, and forests

Range: Endemic (or only found in) Florida, Georgia, and Alabama. In Georgia, it can be found only in the southern portion of the state in the coastal plains area.

Food: Herbivores (plant eaters) that feed on various types of plants like grasses, shrubs, flowers, and roots

Den: Nest is set in a cavity area that is off the main burrow. Nests are filled with grasses and other plant material that has been shaped into a ball.

Young: Most births take place in spring or later in the summer throughout the months of July and August. Up to 4 pups, 2 inches long, are born at a time. Will become fully independent within a month and will become mature at around 4–6 months.

Predators: Coyotes, foxes, owls, hawks, skunks, weasels, and snakes (predation usually takes place when the gophers are at the surface)

Tracks: Front legs are strong with large claws that aid in digging.

The southeastern pocket gopher is a stocky cylinder or soda can–shaped small mammal with small eyes and ears. They have powerful front feet with large claws. They have golden-penny brown to deep-brown fur on their back. The fur below is paler and buffy gray-colored with hues of lighter browns.

Did you know?

The southern flying squirrel doesn't actually fly! Instead, it uses special folds of skin to glide through the air. They can glide over 100 feet at a time. They have thick paws that aid them in landing. Because they move from tree to tree, they help to spread seeds and fungi.

Size Comparison   Most Active

Southern Flying Squirrel

Glaucomys volans

Size: 9 inches long; weighs 2–3 ounces

Habitat: Forests with older trees

Range: They are found statewide in Georgia and throughout the eastern US and parts of Mexico.

Food: Nuts, berries, acorns, small birds, mice, insects, and mushrooms

Den: They make nests in tree hollows. They will also use abandoned woodpecker holes and human-made nest boxes or birdhouses. They line the nest with chewed bark, grasses, moss, and feathers.

Young: 2–3 young (kits) are born per litter; they drink milk from the mother for around 70 days and will be fully independent around 4 months and mature at around a year old.

Predators: Small hawks, foxes, owls, martens (weasel-like mammals), and weasels

Tracks: Tracks are rare because they spend most of their time in trees.

The southern flying squirrel is a grayish-brown nocturnal (active at night) animal that glides through the air from tree to tree. The patagium, or skin fold, stretches from their ankles to their wrist, allowing them to "fly." (People have even built similar "squirrel suits" to glide with, and they've worked!) During winter months, flying squirrels share cavities with others.

The Southern Flying Squirrel does not often leave tracks.

Did you know?

The spotted skunk is the only skunk in the US that can climb trees. Sometimes it will climb trees to knock down beehives and feed on the honeycombs. Skunks are most well-known for the oily, smelly substance that they can spray from their rear-end area. When spraying, they can usually hit what they're aiming for!

Size Comparison   Most Active   Track Size

1¼"

46

Spotted Skunk

Spilogale putorius

Size: 16–24 inches long; weighs 1–4 pounds

Habitat: Forests, grasslands, shrublands, woodlands, and fields

Range: Found in northern and eastern Georgia, as well as much of the eastern United States and in areas of Canada and Mexico

Food: Omnivore (eats both plants and animals); corn, rabbits, salamanders, insects, mice, fruit, birds, and bird eggs

Den: Dens are commonly made above the ground, in a hole or a rock crevice, or under a hollow log or stump. Will utilize multiple dens throughout home range for various purposes. While they can and will dig their own dens, they will also use abandoned dens made by other animals.

Young: Around 3–6 kits are born blind with the spotted black-and-white pattern. They are independent within 3 months and reach reproductive age around 11 months.

Predators: Owls, hawks, bobcats, coyotes. Often injured by pet dogs

Tracks: Front feet are ¾ inch long and hind feet are 1¼ inches long. Both front and hind have five toe pads.

The spotted skunk is a small stocky animal with short legs. They have coarse, long fur that is patterned with black-and-white spots and stripes. They are smaller than the striped skunk.

Did you know?

The star-nosed mole has a special sensory organ. Also known as an Eimer's organ, the mole's "nose" has over 20,000 receptors that allow the mole to navigate. While this animal is a great digger, it's also a decent swimmer and can stay underwater for 30 seconds or more. They have the ability to smell underwater, by using air bubbles to get the scent from submerged objects.

Size Comparison   Most Active   Track Size

1"

Star-nosed Mole

Condylura cristata

Size: 7–11½ inches long; weighs 1–3 ounces

Habitat: Forests, wetlands, meadows, and mountains

Range: Can be found in the eastern parts of North America. In Georgia, it is found in the mountainous areas of northern Georgia as well as along the coastal plain.

Food: Carnivore (meat eater) whose diet consist of insects, small fish, crustaceans, and shelled aquatic animals like clams and snails

Den: Nest cavities are built near stumps or logs, about 5–7 inches long and 4–5 inches high. In areas that are damp, nests are built on a raised area that is drier.

Young: A litter of 2–7 pups is born each year. Pups are born blind and without fur. They are independent within a month and able to reproduce within 10 months.

Predators: Hawks, owls, minks, foxes, weasels, snakes, cats, and sometimes bullfrogs and large fish

Tracks: Four feet that face outward with claws that help in digging underground tunnels

The star-nosed mole has black/slate-gray fur and large forefeet equipped with claws that aid in digging. Both sets of feet (fore and hind feet) face outward. They have a long, hairy tail. Their snout or nose has over 20 pink, tentacle-like organs that they use to navigate and find food. Active throughout the winter; in areas where the ground freezes, they will hunt in water.

Did you know?

Tricolored bats got their name because of the three different colors of fur on their back: dark gray on the bottom, golden-brown in the middle, and brown or earth-tone red on the top. The tricolored bat is the smallest bat in Georgia!

Size Comparison   Most Active   Hibernates

Tricolored Bat

Perimyotis subflavus

Size: 3–3½ inches long; wingspan is 8⅓–10⅓ inches; weighs ¹⁄₁₀–¾ ounce or about as much as a quarter

Habitat: Forests, caves, urban (city) areas, grasslands, and orchards

Range: Widespread across the eastern and central US as far west as Texas. It can be found throughout Georgia.

Food: Mosquitoes, beetles, ants, moths, and cicadas

Den: Roost in trees, buildings, culverts (sewage drains), caves, and in Spanish moss. Females will roost in colonies of 25 or more individuals. Males are solitary and do not have bachelor colonies like other bat species. Bats mate in the fall and give birth in the spring.

Young: Pups are born blind and furless in June and July. Pups learn to fly 3 weeks after birth, and within a month they are able to hunt for themselves. They are mature by their first fall but will not usually mate until their second fall.

Predators: Owls, raccoons, snakes, and hawks

Tracks: Though they are rarely on the ground to leave a track, it would show as one thumbprint from the forearm and a hind footprint.

Tricolored bats are a golden hue of yellowish and brown fur. Single hairs are darkly shaded at the bottom, yellow hued in the midsection, and brown at the tip. This is the reason for the name "tricolored." During the winter they hibernate in caves, mines, and rock crevices. In Georgia and other areas with a lack of caves or mines, they hibernate in roadside culverts.

The tricolored bat does not often leave tracks.

Did you know?

The opossum is the only marsupial native to the US. Marsupials are a special group of animals that are most well-known for their pouches, which they use to carry their young. When frightened, young opossums will play dead (called playing possum) and adults will show their teeth and hiss or run away.

Size Comparison   Most Active   Track Size

2½"

Virginia Opossum

Didelphis virginiana

Size: 22–45 inches long; weighs 4–8 pounds

Habitat: Forests, woodlands, meadows, and suburban areas

Range: They are found throughout Georgia; they are found throughout the eastern US, Canada, and also in Mexico and Costa Rica.

Food: Eggs, small mammals, garbage, insects, worms, birds, fruit, and occasionally small reptiles and amphibians

Den: They den in hollow trees, abandoned animal burrows, and buildings.

Young: A litter of 6–20 young (joeys) are born blind and without fur; their limbs are not fully formed. Young will climb from the birthing area into the mother's pouch and stay until 8 weeks old; they then alternate between the mother's pouch and her back for 4 weeks. At 12 weeks they are independent.

Predators: Hawks, owls, pet cats and dogs, coyotes, and bobcats

Tracks: The front feet are 2 inches long and around 1½ inches wide and resemble a child's hands; the hind feet are 2½ inches long and around 2¼ inches wide; they have fingers in front with a fifth finger that acts as a thumb.

The Virginia opossum has long gray-and-black fur; the face is white, and the tail is pink to gray and furless. Opossums have long claws.

Did you know?

When they first emerge, a deer's antlers are covered in a special skin called velvet. Deer can run up to 40 miles per hour and can jump over 8 feet vertically (high) and over 15 feet horizontally (across).

Size Comparison   Most Active   Track Size

3"

White-tailed Deer

Odocoileus virginianus

Size: 4–6 feet long; 3–4 feet tall at front shoulder; weighs 114–308 pounds

Habitat: Forest edges, brushy fields, woody farmlands, prairies, and swamps

Range: They are found throughout Georgia and throughout the US except for much of the Southwest; they are also found in southern Canada and into South America.

Food: Fruits, grass, tree shrubs, nuts, and bark

Den: Deer do not den but will bed down in tall grasses and shrubby areas.

Young: Deer usually give birth to twins (fawns) that are 3–6 pounds in late May to June. The fawns are born with spots; this coloration helps them hide in vegetation. Young become independent at 1–2 years.

Predators: Wolves, coyotes, bears, bobcats, and humans

Tracks: Both front and hind feet have two teardrop- or comma-shaped toes.

Crepuscular (active at dawn and dusk), white-tailed deer have big brown eyes with eye rings and a long snout with a black, glossy nose. The males have antlers, which fall off each year. All deer have a white tail that they flash upward when alarmed. Deer molt or change fur color twice a year. They sport rusty-brown fur in the summer; in early fall, they transition to winter coats that are grayish brown in color.

Did you know?

The American goldfinch helps restore habitats by spreading seeds. The goldfinch gets its color from a pigment called a carotenoid (say it, cuh-rot-en-oid) in the seeds it eats. It can even feed upside down by using its feet to bring seeds to its mouth.

Nest Type

American Goldfinch

Spinus tristis

Size: 4½–5 inches long; wingspan of 9 inches; weighs about half an ounce

Habitat: Grasslands, meadows, suburban areas, and wetlands

Range: Found throughout much of Georgia year-round; in summer, they can be found in far northern parts of the state; found all over the US

Food: Seeds of plants and trees; sometimes feeds on insects; loves thistle seeds at birdfeeders

Nesting: Goldfinches build nests in late June.

Nest: Cup-shaped nests are built a couple of feet above-ground out of roots and plant fibers.

Eggs: 2–7 eggs with a bluish-white tint

Young: Young (chicks) hatch around 15 days after being laid; they hatch without feathers and weigh only a gram. Chicks learn to fly after around 11–15 days. Young become mature at around 11 months old.

Predators: Garter snakes, blue jays, American kestrels, and cats

Migration: Most goldfinches stay in Georgia for the winter, though birds in the northern part of the state migrate south.

During the summer, American goldfinch males are brightly colored with golden-yellow feathers and an orange beak. They have black wings with white wing bars. The crown (top) of the head is black. In winter, they molt, and the males look more like the females. Females are always greenish yellow with hints of yellow around the head.

Did you know?

Anhingas often soar high up in the sky in groups called "kettles," often with raptors. The anhinga is less buoyant (floats less easily) than other birds, so its body sits lower in the water with its head and neck sticking out, making it easy to mistake for a snake. This is why it is sometimes called the snake bird.

Nest Type   Migrates

Anhinga
Anhinga anhinga

Size: 28½–37½ inches long; wingspan of 43 inches; weighs 45–48 ounces

Habitat: Shallow areas of freshwater marshes, swamps, mangroves, lagoons, and rivers

Range: Can be found year-round in the eastern coastal areas of the US. In Georgia, many are year-round residents along the coast and extreme South. Inland residents can be seen during the breeding season.

Food: Mostly fish, but they also feed on aquatic (water-living) insects, crawfish, and shrimp. Sometimes they will take on snakes, alligator hatchlings, and baby turtles.

Nesting: Nesting takes place in colonies, or rookeries, of other water-loving birds. Parents share care duties.

Nest: Platform nests are constructed mostly by the female with the male supplying sticks and twigs; the inside is usually lined with grasses and leaves.

Eggs: 2–5 palish-white-to-blue eggs about 2–2½ inches long and 1½ inches wide

Young: Eggs hatch 25–30 days after laying. Chicks are born with eyes open and featherless. Young will leap out of the nest in the presence of danger.

Predators: Snakes, squirrels, owls, common ravens, blue jays, red-bellied woodpeckers, and a variety of hawks

Migration: Most are year-round residents that will migrate short distances to areas in Florida or Mexico.

Males are black with whitish to silver streaking on the back and wings. Juveniles and females have a light-brown-to-tan head and body. Both sexes have orange-yellow feet, legs, and bill.

Did you know?

The bald eagle is an endangered species success story! The bald eagle was once endangered due to a pesticide called DDT that weakened eggshells and caused them to crack early. Through the banning of DDT and other conservation efforts, the bald eagle population recovered, and it was removed from the Endangered Species List in July of 2007.

Nest Type   Migrates

Bald Eagle

Haliaeetus leucocephalus

Size: 3½ feet long; wingspan of 6½–8 feet; weighs 8–14 pounds

Habitat: Forests and tree stands (small forests) near river edges, lakes, seashores, and wetlands

Range: They are a resident bird throughout Georgia; they are found throughout much of the US.

Food: Fish, waterfowl (ducks), rabbits, squirrels, muskrats, and deer carcasses; will steal food from other eagles or osprey

Nesting: Eagles have lifelong partners that begin nesting in fall, laying eggs between November–February.

Nest: They build a large nest out of sticks, high up in trees; the nest can be over 5 feet wide and over 6 feet tall, often shaped like an upside-down cone.

Eggs: 1–3 white eggs

Young: Young (chicks) will hatch around 35 days; young will leave the nest around 12 weeks. It takes up to 5 years for eagles to get that iconic look!

Predators: Few; collisions with cars sometimes occur.

Migration: They are short-distance migrators, usually to coastal areas; in Georgia, many eagles do not migrate at all.

Adult bald eagles have a dark-brown body, a white head and tail, and a golden-yellow beak. Juvenile eagles are mostly brown at first, but their color pattern changes over their first few years. A bald eagle can use its wings as oars to propel itself across bodies of water.

Did you know?
The barred owl has dark brown eyes; many other owls have yellow eyes. Barred owls, like other owls, have special structures on their primary feathers that allow them to fly silently through the air.

Nest Type

Barred Owl

Strix varia

Size: 17–20 inches long; wingspan of 3½ feet; weighs 2 pounds

Habitat: Forested areas, near floodplains of lakes and rivers

Range: They can be found throughout the state of Georgia; they are found throughout the eastern US and southern Canada, with scattered populations throughout the Pacific Northwest.

Food: Squirrels, rabbits, and mice; will also prey on birds and aquatic animals like frogs, fish, and crawfish

Nesting: Courtship starts in late fall; nesting starts in winter

Nest: They use hollow trees; they will also use abandoned nests of other animals and human-made nest structures.

Eggs: 2–4 white eggs with a rough shell

Young: Young (chicks) hatch between 27 and 33 days; they have white down feathers and leave the nest around 5 weeks after hatching. They are fully independent at around 6 months and fully mature at around 2 years.

Predators: Great horned owls, raccoons, weasels, and sometimes northern goshawks feed on eggs and young in the nest.

Migration: Barred owls do not migrate.

The barred owl is a medium-size bird with dark rings highlighting the face. Their feathers are brown and grayish, often with streaking or a bar-like pattern. They have no ear tufts and have a rounded head with a yellow beak and brown eyes. They can easily be identified by their call: "Who cooks for you, who cooks for you all?"

Did you know?

Kingfishers inspired human technology! Bullet trains around the world are designed after the kingfisher's beak, which allows them to dive into water without a splash. This design was used in bullet trains to allow them to enter into tunnels without making a large booming sound. This process of modeling human technology after animal features is called biomimicry.

Nest Type   Migrates

Belted Kingfisher

Megaceryle alcyon

Size: 11–13¾ inches long; wingspan is 19–24 inches; weighs 5–6 ounces

Habitat: Forests and grassland areas near rivers, ponds, lakes

Range: Year-round resident of Georgia as well as most of the United States; in other areas of the US, it is either a seasonal visitor during the breeding or nonbreeding seasons.

Food: Mostly carnivorous; mostly fish and other aquatic animals such as crawfish and frogs, and occasionally other birds, mammals, and berries

Nesting: Nests are in the form of upward-sloped burrows that are dug in soft banks on or near water. (The upward slopes prevent flooding.)

Nest: Females and males select the nest site together; male does most of the digging.

Eggs: 5–8 white, smooth, glossy eggs are laid per clutch (group of eggs).

Young: Chicks are born featherless with pink skin, closed eyes, and a dark bill. They receive care from both parents. Chicks leave the nest after about 28 days.

Predators: Snakes, hawks, and mammals

Migration: Mostly a resident bird; in some areas, will migrate south during nonbreeding season

The belted kingfisher is bluish gray on top; the bottom half is white with a blue/gray belt or band. The wings have white spots on them. Unlike most other birds, the kingfisher female has a different pattern than the male. Females have a second reddish-brown or rusty-orange band on their belly.

Did you know?
Turkey vultures have something most birds don't: a good sense of smell. Black vultures take advantage of this by soaring in circles above a turkey vulture and waiting until it finds food. Then they join in on the meal. A trick to tell them apart: Black vultures are all black with white wing tips. Turkey vultures make a black "T" shape and have light gray undersides on the wings/tail.

Black Vulture/Turkey Vulture

Coragyps atratus/Cathartes aura

Size: Black: 23½–27 inches long; wingspan is 53½–59 inches; weighs 56½–78 ounces. Turkey: 25¼–32 inches long; wingspan is 66–70 inches; weighs 70 ounces

Habitat: Forests, woodland edges, cities, farmland

Range: Year-round in Georgia

Food: Carrion (dead animals) like deer, snakes, feral hogs, coyotes, and armadillos. Black vultures may kill smaller animals if given the chance.

Nesting: Black: Caves, tree cavities, brush piles, abandoned buildings in large groups. Turkey: Secluded caves, cliff ledges, hollow trees, abandoned nests

Nest: Black: Existing cavities in nature. Turkey: A simple "scrape" nest of discarded plants or wood

Eggs: Black: 1–3 speckled white eggs; Turkey: 1–3 creamy-white, speckled eggs

Young: Black: Chicks fledge after 10 weeks but depend on their parents for several months. Turkey: Chicks fledge 70 days after hatching and are independent a week or so afterward.

Predators: Raccoons, opossums, and foxes prey on eggs. Snakes, eagles, hawks, and owls may attack juveniles or sick or injured adults. Healthy adults are rarely prey.

Migration: Black: May migrate short distances. Turkey: Those in the northern US migrate south.

Black vultures are all black with white wing tips. Turkey vultures look all black, but up close, they are different shades of light gray and brown. Turkey vultures have a red head.

Did you know?

Canada geese sometimes travel over 600 miles in a day. They fly in a V formation, which allows them to travel long distances without stopping because they can switch positions. As the lead bird gets tired, it drops to the back of the line and a new bird leads. The V formation helps them communicate and helps prevent collisions.

Nest Type

Migrates

Canada Goose
Branta canadensis

Size: 2–3½ feet long; wingspan of 5–6 feet; weighs 6½–20 pounds

Habitat: Ponds, marshes, lakes, parks, and farm fields

Range: They can be found throughout Georgia as residents; they are widespread in the rest of the US.

Food: Omnivores; grasses, aquatic insects, seeds, and some crops, like corn or alfalfa

Nesting: March to April

Nest: Nests are made on the ground, on elevated areas near the water, or sometimes on a muskrat mound. Nest sites are picked with protection in mind; areas that have clear views and vantage points are more likely to be used.

Eggs: 2–8 cream-colored eggs that are 3 inches long and about 2½ inches wide

Young: Goslings hatch about a month after being laid. They are born with yellow down feathers that they lose as they get older. At the time of hatching, they can swim and walk.

Predators: Mink, raccoons, foxes, dogs, and great horned owls

Migration: A large portion will stay and winter in Georgia, while others will fly farther south.

The Canada goose is recognizable by its famous honk and body pattern of brown feathers with a black neck, head, bill, and even feet. They have white cheek feathers.

Did you know?

The double-crested cormorant does not have oil glands like other aquatic birds; this is why you will see it on a rock or post with its wings spread: it's drying itself off. The cormorant's bill curves at the end, while the anhinga, a similar species that is often confused with a double-crested cormorant, has a pointed, straight-top bill.

Nest Type   Migrates

Double-crested Cormorant

Nannopterum auritum

Size: 26–35 inches long; wingspan of 45–48½ inches; weighs 2½–3 pounds

Habitat: Freshwater lakes, rivers, swamps, coastal waters

Range: They can be found across North America. In Georgia, they can be found statewide.

Food: Carnivores; fish, insects, snails, and crawfish

Nesting: April to August; male chooses the nest site before finding a female. Nest in groups with other water birds

Nest: Veteran parents may repair an old nest. Otherwise, they build a new nest on the ground or in a tree. Nests are made of sticks and lined with grass. Nests can be as wide as 3 feet and over 1½ feet tall.

Eggs: On average, 4 light-bluish-white eggs are laid at a time.

Young: Young chicks (shaglets) usually hatch in 25–28 days; they can swim immediately after hatching.

Predators: Eggs are vulnerable to raccoons, gulls, jays, foxes, and coyotes. Adults and chicks are preyed on by coyotes, foxes, raccoons, eagles, and great horned owls.

Migration: Northern populations migrate south in winter.

Adults have black feathers and topaz-colored eyes, with an orange bill, throat, and face area; they have black feet that are webbed, like a duck's. The tail is short. During breeding season, adults may have a "double crest" of black feathers or sometimes white depending on the location. This is where they get the name double-crested cormorant. Young are all brown or black.

Did you know?

Have you ever heard of a bird ordering someone to drink tea? Well, that's exactly what the eastern towhee does with its song of "DRINK your tea!" There are some towhees in southern Georgia and Florida that have white eyes instead of red eyes like other eastern towhees.

Nest Type

Migrates

Eastern Towhee

Pipilo erythrophthalmus

Size: 7–8½ inches long; wingspan of 8–11 inches; weighs 1–2 ounces

Habitat: Open woodlands, forest edges, meadows, prairies, gardens, parks, and suburban areas

Range: Eastern towhees occur throughout Georgia, as well as in the eastern United States and southeast Canada.

Food: Omnivores that feed on seeds and fruits, as well as insects and other invertebrates. They will sometimes eat snakes, lizards, and small amphibians.

Nesting: Nesting begins in spring and continues through the summer. The female constructs the nest.

Nest: Low in bushes or under shrubs on the ground. Nests are cup shaped and made out of woody plant material. The inside of the nest is lined with grasses, thin roots, and sometimes fur from animals.

Eggs: Clutch (group of eggs) size is 2–6 eggs in a variety of colors, including cream, grayish pink, white, speckled brown, red, and purple.

Young: Chicks are born blind and bald, except for a few areas with down feathers. Chicks receive food from both parents. Fledging takes place 10–12 days after hatching, but they will receive care for at least another month.

Predators: Snakes, hawks, and owls

Migration: Northern populations spend winter in the southern US.

Males have a dark-black head, tail, and upper body, while females are chocolate brown. Immature towhees are brown throughout. Both adults have burnt-orange or clay-colored sides and a white belly with white edges that run alongside the tail.

Did you know?

The catbird can make over 100 different types of sounds, including one song that can last well over 5 minutes. Catbirds are intelligent; they are one of the few species of songbirds that can recognize and remove brown-headed cowbird eggs when they are abandoned in their nests. Brown-headed cowbirds will lay their eggs in the nests of other birds and make them raise their young.

Nest Type

Migrates

Gray Catbird

Dumetella carolinensis

Size: 8¼–9½ inches long; wingspan of 8¾–11¾ inches; weighs ¾–2 ounces

Habitat: Shrubs, urban (city) areas, vine tangles, and thickets

Range: Gray catbirds can be found in most parts of North America east of the Rocky Mountains throughout various times of the year. In Georgia, they are year-round residents in the southeastern area and migrate to more northern areas during breeding season.

Food: Ants, flies, beetles, moths, grasshoppers, caterpillars, and spiders. They also eat various fruits and berries.

Nesting: Starts in April and goes to early August. The female builds the nest, and the male will supply materials sometimes. The male guards the nest while the female incubates the eggs. Both care for chicks.

Nest: Females build cup nests with twigs, mud, bark, and straw, lined with grass, fur, and pine needles.

Eggs: Clutch size is 3–6 eggs that are teal or turquoise green.

Young: Chicks are born 12–14 days after laying. At hatching, they are naked except for spots of dark down feathers and have their eyes closed. Chicks leave the nest at around 10 days. They receive care for another 12 days or so. They can reproduce at 1 year.

Predators: Pet cats and dogs, foxes, skunks, coyotes, and raptors

Migration: In fall, they migrate to more southern areas, including Texas. During breeding season, they migrate north.

Catbirds are medium-size songbirds. They are slate gray with a black tail. They have a small cinnamon- to rust-colored patch at the base of their tail. Their head is gray with a black cap.

75

Did you know?

The great blue heron is the largest and most common heron species in Georgia. A heron's eye color changes as it ages. The eyes start out gray but transition to yellow over time. Great blue herons swallow their prey whole.

Nest Type   Migrates

Great Blue Heron

Ardea herodias

Size: 3–4½ feet long; wingspan of 6–7 feet; weighs 5–7 pounds

Habitat: Lakes, ponds, rivers, marshes, lagoons, wetlands, and coastal areas like beaches

Range: They can be found throughout Georgia, as well as the entire United States and down into Mexico.

Food: Fish, rats, crabs, shrimp, grasshoppers, crawfish, other birds, small mammals, snakes, and lizards

Nesting: May to August

Nest: 2–3 feet across and saucer shaped; often grouped in large rookeries (colonies) in tall trees along the water's edge. Nests are built out of sticks and are often located in dead trees more than 100 feet above the ground; nests are used year after year.

Eggs: 3–7 pale bluish eggs

Young: Chicks will hatch after 28 days of incubation; young will stay in the nest for around 10 weeks. They reach reproductive maturity at just under 2 years.

Predators: Eagles, crows, gulls, raccoons, bears, and hawks

Migration: Populations in northern areas will fly south to southern states, the Caribbean, and Central America.

The great blue heron is a large wading bird with blue and gray upper body feathers; the belly area is white. They have long yellow legs that they use to stalk prey in the water. Great blue herons are famous for stalking prey at the water's edge; their specially adapted feet keep them from sinking into the mud!

Did you know?

A great horned owl can exert a crushing force of over 300 pounds with its talons. Despite its name, the great horned owls doesn't have horns at all. Instead, the obvious tufts on its head are made of feathers. Scientists aren't sure exactly how they function, but it may help them stay hidden.

Nest Type

Great Horned Owl

Bubo virginianus

Size: Up to 23 inches long; wingspan of 45 inches; weighs 3 pounds

Habitat: Woods; swamps; desert edges; as well as heavily populated areas such as cities, suburbs, and parks

Range: They are found throughout Georgia and the continent of North America.

Food: They eat a variety of foods, but mostly mammals. Sometimes they eat other birds as well.

Nesting: They have lifelong partnerships, with nesting season starting in early winter; egg-laying starts in mid-January to February.

Nest: Nests are found 20–50 feet off the ground. They tend to reuse nests from other raptors or hollowed-out trees.

Eggs: The female lays 2–4 whitish eggs. Eggs are incubated for around 30 days.

Young: Young can fly at around 9 weeks old. The parents care for and feed young for several months.

Predators: Young owls are preyed upon by foxes, coyotes, bears, and opossums. As adults, they are rarely attacked by other birds of prey, such as golden eagles and goshawks.

Migration: Great horned owls are not regular migrators, but some individuals will travel south during the winter.

They are bulky birds with large ear tufts, a rusty brown-to-grayish face with a black border, and large bright eyes. The body color tends to be brown; the wing pattern is checkered with an intermingled dark brown. The chest and belly areas are light brown and have white bars.

Did you know?

When viewed straight-on, the yellow portion on the mallard's bill resembles a cartoon dog's head. Most domesticated ducks share the mallard as their ancestor. Mallard feathers are waterproof; they use oil from the preen gland beneath their feathers to help aid in repelling water. Mallards are the most common duck in the United States and Georgia.

Nest Type   Migrates

Mallard

Anas platyrhynchos

Size: 24 inches long; wingspan of 36 inches; weighs 2½–3 pounds

Habitat: Lakes, ponds, rivers, and marshes

Range: They are found throughout Georgia; the population stretches across the United States and Canada into Mexico and as far up as central Alaska.

Food: Insects, worms, snails, aquatic vegetation, sedge seeds, grasses, snails, and wild rice

Nesting: April to August

Nest: The nest is constructed on the ground, usually near a body of water.

Eggs: 9–13 eggs

Young: Eggs hatch 26–28 days after being laid. The ducklings are fully feathered and have the ability to swim at the time of hatching. Ducklings are cared for until they're 2–3 months old and reach reproductive maturity at 1 year old.

Predators: Humans, crows, mink, coyotes, raccoons, and snapping turtles

Migration: After breeding season, a lot of the population will migrate south; others will stay in familiar areas that have adequate food and shelter.

Male mallards are gray with an iridescent green head with a tinge of purple spotting, a white line along the collar, rusty-brown chest, yellow bill, and orange legs and feet. Females are dull brown with a yellow bill, a bluish area near the tail, and orange feet.

Did you know?

Cardinals are very territorial and will sometimes attack their own reflection thinking that another cardinal has entered its territory. The early bird gets the worm, and cardinals are some of the first birds active in the morning.

Nest Type

Northern Cardinal

Cardinalis cardinalis

Size: 8–9 inches long; wingspan of 12 inches

Habitat: Hardwood forests, urban areas, orchards, backyards, and fields

Range: They are found throughout Georgia, as well as the eastern and midwestern parts of the United States.

Food: Seeds, fruits, insects, spiders, and centipedes

Nesting: March to August

Nest: The cup-shaped nest is built by females in thick foliage, usually at least 1 foot off the ground. It can be 3 inches tall and 4 inches wide.

Eggs: The female lays 2–5 off-white eggs with a variety of colored speckles

Young: About 2 weeks after eggs are laid, chicks hatch with their eyes closed and mostly naked, aside from sparsely placed down feathers.

Predators: Hawks, owls, and squirrels

Migration: Cardinals do not migrate.

Northern cardinal males are bright-red birds with a black face. Females are a washed-out red or brown. Both males and females have a crest (tuft of feathers on the head), and orange beaks and grayish legs. Cardinals can be identified by their laser-gun-like call.

Did you know?

Northern mockingbirds get their name from their ability to mimic or "mock" sounds of other birds, organisms, and even machines. They can sing 40 to more than 200 songs depending on region. Mockingbirds are brave and will defend their nest from larger birds like raptors. When danger is present, mockingbirds can form an allegiance with neighbors to protect the shared area.

Nest Type

Northern Mockingbird

Mimus polyglottos

Size: 8–10 inches long; wingspan of 12–14 inches; weighs 1½–2 ounces

Habitat: Hardwood forests, urban areas, parks, orchards, backyards, and fields

Range: They are found throughout Georgia, as well as the rest of the United States; in the northern US, they are migrants.

Food: Omnivore that feeds on seeds, fruits, insects, earthworms, and sometimes lizards

Nesting: Spring to early fall

Nest: The cup-shaped nest is built by both males and females, with the male doing most of the building. The nest is composed of twigs with the inside lined with dead leaves, grass, moss, and manmade materials.

Eggs: 3–5 blue-to-green eggs speckled with brownish-red

Young: About 2 weeks after the mother lays the eggs, chicks hatch. They're born nearly naked and with their eyes closed.

Predators: Domesticated cats, crows, snakes, blue jays, hawks, owls, and squirrels

Migration: Most northern mockingbirds are permanent residents, though some will migrate south during really harsh winters.

Mockingbirds are medium-size grayish songbirds. They have a white belly and dark gray wings with a bold white patch. Mockingbirds have a long dark-gray tail with bright white outer feathers.

Did you know?

The osprey is nicknamed the "fish hawk" because it is the only hawk in North America that mainly eats live fish. An osprey will rotate its catch to put it in line with its body, pointing head first, which allows for less resistance in flight as the air travels over the fish.

Nest Type

Migrates

Osprey

Pandion haliaetus

Size: 21–23 inches long; wingspan of 59–71 inches; weighs 3–4½ pounds

Habitat: Near lakes, ponds, rivers, swamps, and reservoirs

Range: Most of Georgia year-round, and throughout the US and Canada and Alaska

Food: Feeds mostly on fish; they sometimes eat mammals, birds, and reptiles if there are few fish.

Nesting: For ospreys that migrate, egg-laying happens in April and May. The female will take on most of the incubation of the eggs, as well as the jobs of keeping the offspring warm and providing protection.

Nest: Platform nests are constructed out of twigs and sticks. Nests are constructed on trees, snags, or human-made objects like cellular towers and telephone poles.

Eggs: The mother lays 1–3 cream-colored eggs; they have splotches of various shades of brown and pinkish red on them.

Young: Chicks hatch after around 36 days and have brown-and-white down feathers. Osprey fledge around 50–55 days after hatching and will receive care from parents for another 2 months or so.

Predators: Owls, eagles, foxes, skunks, raccoons, snakes

Migration: Ospreys migrate south to wintering areas in the fall.

Ospreys are raptors, and they have a brown upper body and white lower body. The wings are brown on the outside and white on the underside with brown spotting and streaks towards the edge. The head is white with a brown band that goes through the eye area, highlighting the yellow eyes.

Did you know?

Painted buntings are the only birds in the United States that have a solid red breast and belly, and a solid blue head. Males do not get their iconic plumage until after their second year. Sometimes painted buntings will steal prey from spiders and their webs.

Nest Type

Migrates

Painted Bunting

Passerina ciris

Size: 5½ inches long; wingspan of 8¾ inches; weighs ½ ounce

Habitat: Hardwood forests, urban areas, orchards, coastal areas, backyards, and fields

Range: They are found in the southern and eastern parts of Georgia, and the eastern and midwestern US.

Food: Omnivores; diet depends on the season. They feed on seeds, snails, insects, spiders, and caterpillars.

Nesting: March to early August. Males arrive first and pick a breeding area to defend. Both birds pick a nesting area.

Nest: The cup-shaped nest is built by females in thick foliage at least 3–6 feet off the ground. It can be 2½ inches tall and 3 inches wide. The nest is woven out of leaves, bark, twigs, spiderwebs, and grasses. It is lined with grasses and hair.

Eggs: 3–4 gray or blue-white eggs with brown or gray spots.

Young: Chicks hatch 12 days after eggs are laid; they are born mostly naked, with eyes closed. Both parents feed the young. The chicks fledge around day 12 but will receive care for at least 3 more weeks. Females may raise two broods a year.

Predators: Hawks, owls, and squirrels

Migration: They migrate at night to warmer areas in fall and return in early spring to breeding areas.

Male painted buntings are a brightly colored mix of blues, greens, reds, and yellows. Females and juveniles are dullish or semi-bright yellow to olive green with eye rings.

Did you know?

The peregrine falcon is the fastest diving bird in the world. A peregrine falcon can reach speeds over 200 miles per hour (mph) when diving. To aid in diving and maneuvering in the air, like most other birds, peregrine falcons have a third eyelid called a nictitating membrane that helps to keep out debris and wind.

Peregrine Falcon

Falco peregrinus

Size: 14–19½ inches long; wingspan of 39–43 inches; weighs 1–3½ pounds

Habitat: Hardwood forests, coastal areas and marshes, urban areas, orchards, backyards, and fields

Range: They are found throughout the US and much of Georgia during migration. There are a few permanent residents in the Atlanta area and along the coast.

Food: Carnivores, feeding on pigeons, songbirds, aquatic birds, rodents, and sometimes bats

Nesting: February to March. Pairs mate for life and reuse nests. The female chooses a nest site and will scrape a shallow hole in loose soil or sand. Nests are usually on cliff edges or tall buildings. Sometimes they even use abandoned nests of other large birds.

Nest: Shallow ground scrapes about 8–9 inches wide and 2 inches deep with no extra nesting materials added.

Eggs: 3–5 off-white-to-brown eggs speckled brown or purple

Young: 30 days after eggs are laid, chicks (or eyas) will hatch with eyes closed and covered in off-white down.

Predators: Great horned owls, golden eagles, and humans

Migration: Northern and central populations migrate for breeding. Coastal populations are less likely to migrate.

The female is slightly larger than the male. Peregrine falcons have gray wings with black to gray bar-like marks and deep black wing tips. The breast and belly areas are covered with black-to-brown horizontal streaks or bars. They have a black head and black head and black marks below the eyes. The neck is white. The beak, legs, eye rings, and feet are yellow.

Did you know?

The red-tailed hawk is the most abundant hawk in North America. (Look for it on powerlines!) The red-tailed hawk's scream is the sound effect that you hear when soaring eagles are shown in movies. Eagles do not screech like hawks, so filmmakers use hawk calls instead!

Nest Type

Red-tailed Hawk (RT)/ Red-shouldered Hawk (RS)

Buteo jamaicensis / Buteo lineatus

Size: RT: 19–25 inches long; wingspan of 47–57 inches; weighs 2½–4 pounds. RS: 16½–24 inches long; wingspan of 37–43 inches; weighs around 1 pound

Habitat: RT: Deserts, woodlands, fields. RS: Forests, swamps, grasslands, urban areas

Range: RT: Georgia and throughout North America. RS: Found throughout Georgia and the eastern US; also found on parts of the Pacific Coast

Food: RT: Rodents, birds, reptiles, bats, and insects. RS: Small mammals, lizards, snakes, crawfish, songbirds

Nesting: Hawks mate for life; nesting starts in March.

Nest: RT: Both parents build a large cup-shaped nest (can be 6 feet high and 3 feet wide), made of sticks and branches. RS: Both male and female build a cup-shaped nest 20 feet off the ground.

Eggs: RT: White with colored blotches; RS: Off-white or slightly blue with varied markings

Young: RT: Young hatch after 30 days. They can fly at 5–6 weeks. RS: Chicks can fly after 5–6 weeks.

Predators: RT: Owls and crows. RS: Snakes, mammals, and owls

Migration: Both birds are year-round residents of Georgia.

Red-tailed hawks are named for their rusty-red tails! They have brown heads and a creamy, light-brown chest with a band of brown streaking. Red-shouldered hawks have a reddish-brown head and back, with rusty undersides with white barring across the belly.

Did you know?

Spoonbills have feathers on their head until they reach maturity around 3 years or so; that's when they get the iconic bald head. Spoonbills also hatch with a straight bill, which later changes to the famous spoon-like shape as they get older. Their nostrils are located high up on their bill, near the eyes. This enables them to breathe while the rest of the bill is underwater.

Nest Type

Roseate Spoonbill

Platalea ajaja

Size: 28–34 inches long; wingspan of 47–50 inches; weighs 2½–4 pounds

Habitat: Shrubby coastal areas, marshes, bays, swamps, mangroves, and mudflats

Range: Found along the Georgia and southeastern US coasts

Food: Mostly carnivorous; feeds on crustaceans, shrimp, aquatic insects, amphibians, and smaller fish

Nesting: Nesting takes place in trees and shrubs near water in colonies with other wading birds. Both parents will incubate the eggs.

Nest: Large and cup shaped, made of branches and stems. Males collect the nest material and the females build the nest in high shady areas.

Eggs: 2–5 off-white-to-green eggs with brown spots

Young: Chicks are born with eyes closed and covered in down feathers, 20–23 days after laying. They leave the nest at 35 days and are independent at 7 weeks.

Predators: Eggs and chicks are the most vulnerable to raccoons, coyotes, and hawks. As adults, alligators, coyotes, and humans can be predators (due to illegal hunting).

Migration: Year-round resident of Georgia

Roseate spoonbills are large, pink wading birds. Both male and female adults have a featherless greenish-gray head. The neck, back, and breast are covered in white feathers. The rest of the body is covered in rose-colored feathers. During breeding season, they sport a deep hot-pink-colored shoulder patch. Juveniles are a paler pink and have a head covered with feathers.

Did you know?

The smallest bird that you can find in Georgia is the ruby-throated hummingbird. During migration, male hummingbirds will utilize sapsucker (woodpecker) sap wells to get nutrients because of the lack of flowering plants in early spring. Hummingbirds can achieve 200 wing beats per second.

Nest Type

Migrates

Ruby-throated Hummingbird

Archilochus colubris

Size: 3–3½ inches long; wingspan of 3⅛–4¼ inches; weighs ⅒ of an ounce

Habitat: Forested areas, orchards, gardens, and city parks

Range: They can be found throughout the state of Georgia; they breed in the eastern United States and eastern and central Canada.

Food: Drinks nectar from flowers and eats small insects and spiders

Nesting: March to August

Nest: A walnut-size nest is built in wooded areas, usually 10–20 feet off the ground; nest can be made of grasses, spiderwebs, and other vegetation. Nest is often covered with lichen chips.

Eggs: 2 white eggs

Young: Young (chicks) will start flying around 20 days after hatching.

Predators: Cats, spiders, robber flies, praying mantises, dragonflies, frogs, hawks, falcons, and kites (birds of prey)

Migration: Hummingbirds migrate to Mexico or Central America starting in August.

Ruby-throated hummingbirds are the only species of hummingbirds that nest in the eastern United States. Males have a magnificent ruby-colored throat made of iridescent (shimmering) feathers; males also have green iridescent feathers on their wings. Females are duller in comparison.

Did you know?
White ibises will wash their food to eat. When they find an item that is very muddy, they will dunk it in the water before consuming it. White ibises are very social birds that live and nest in groups or colonies. Often other wading birds, like egrets, will follow behind them when they are foraging because they will stir up food that the egrets eat.

Nest Type   Migrates

White Ibis
Eudocimus albus

Size: 22–24 inches tall; wingspan of 3 feet; weighs 3 pounds

Habitat: Marshes, swamps, mud flats, mangroves, coastal and estuarine areas, ponds, and flooded fields

Range: White ibises can be found along the Atlantic and Gulf coasts of the US. During migration, birds can be found in central and southern Georgia. They can also be found year-round in southern and coastal areas of Georgia.

Food: Carnivores that mostly feed on crawfish, crabs, insects, frogs, lizards, snails, and small fish

Nesting: Takes place in the spring when the female selects the site near water and usually in a shrub or tree branches. Nesting happens in colonies with other wading birds. Both parents provide care to chicks.

Nest: Both adults build a messy platform using vegetation. The nest is about 10 inches wide and 2–4 inches tall.

Eggs: 1–5 creamy to bluish-green eggs with brown spots

Young: Chicks hatch 3 weeks after laying, with eyes closed and covered in down feathers. They fledge around 28 days and become independent at around 7 weeks.

Predators: Crows, raccoons, alligators, snakes, black-crowned night-herons, opossums, owls, and humans

Migration: They arrive in late March to early May and migrate south from September into December.

White ibises are mostly white, except for the black tips of the wings. They have a long reddish-pink bill and legs. The skin around their blue eyes is also pink. Immatures are a marbled brown and white with a paler bill and legs.

Did you know?

Turkeys sometimes fly at night, unlike most birds, and land in trees to roost. Turkeys have some interesting facial features; the red skin growth on a turkey's face above the beak is called a snood, while the growth under the beak is called a wattle. Wild turkeys can have more than 5,000 feathers.

Nest Type

Wild Turkey

Meleagris gallopavo

Size: 3–4 feet long; wingspan of 5 feet; males weigh 16–25 pounds; females weigh 9–11 pounds

Habitat: Woodlands and grasslands

Range: Found throughout Georgia. They also can be found in the eastern US and have been introduced in many western areas of the country.

Food: Grain, snakes, frogs, insects, acorns, berries, and ferns

Nesting: April to September

Nest: The nest is built on the ground using leaves as bedding, in brush or near the base of trees or fallen logs.

Eggs: 10–12 tan eggs with very small reddish-brown spots

Young: Poults (young) hatch about a month after eggs are laid; they will flock with the mother for a year. When young are still unable to fly, the mom will stay on the ground with her poults to provide protection and warmth. When poults grow up, they are known as a hen if they are female, or a gobbler or tom if they are male.

Predators: Humans, foxes, raccoons, owls, eagles, skunks

Migration: Turkeys do not migrate.

A wild turkey is a large bird that is dark brown and black with some iridescent feathers. Males will fan out their tail to attract a mate. When threatened, they will also fan out their tail and rush the predator, sometimes kicking and puncturing prey with the spurs on their feet.

Did you know?

Wood ducks will "mimic" a soccer player when a predator is near their young: they flop! Female wood ducks will fake a broken wing to lure predators away from their young. Wood duck hatchlings must jump from the nest after hatching to reach the water. They can jump 50 feet or more without hurting themselves.

Nest Type

Migrates

Wood Duck

Aix sponsa

Size: 15–20 inches long; wingspan of 30 inches; weighs about 1 pound

Habitat: Swamps, woody ponds, and marshes

Range: They are found throughout Georgia; during the breeding season they're found in the northern parts of the state. Wood ducks are year-long residents in central and southern Georgia; they are also in the eastern US, southern Mexico, the Pacific Northwest, and on the West Coast.

Food: Fruits, nuts, and aquatic vegetation, especially duckweed, sedges, and grasses

Nesting: March to August

Nest: Wood ducks use hollow trees, abandoned woodpecker cavities, and human-made nesting boxes.

Eggs: 8–15 off-white eggs are laid once a year. Sometimes females will lay eggs in another female's nest; this process is called egg dumping.

Young: Eggs hatch about a month after being laid. Chicks will leave the nest after a day and fly within 8 weeks.

Predators: Raccoons, mink, fish, hawks, snapping turtles, owls, humans, and muskrats

Migration: They migrate south in winter and north in spring using the Mississippi flyway.

Wood duck males have a brightly colored crest (tuft of feathers) of iridescent (shimmering) green, red, and purple, with a mahogany (brown) upper breast area and tan bottom. Males also have red eyes. Females are brown to gray. Wood ducks have strong claws that enable them to climb up trees into cavities.

Did you know?

Wood storks are the only species of storks that breed in the US. Wood storks will sometimes steal the nest of another wood stork, throwing the eggs and young out of the nest. While their legs are actually black, oftentimes they look white because they will use the restroom on themselves as a way to keep cool. The white color comes from a chemical called uric acid, which turns into a white paste mixed in with their waste.

Nest Type

Migrates

Wood Stork

Mycteria americana

Size: 33½–45½ inches tall; wingspan of 60–65 inches; weighs about 4–6 pounds

Habitat: Freshwater marshes, mangrove, flooded fields, ponds, lakes, lagoons, streams, swamps, and rivers

Range: The United States has breeding populations in Florida, Georgia, and North and South Carolina.

Food: Mostly carnivores; fish, rodents, crawfish, turtles, crabs, aquatic insects, snakes, baby alligators, and frogs. They sometimes eat plant material.

Nesting: March to August, they nest colonially in trees.

Nest: Platform nest is built by both male and female using twigs and sticks. The inside is lined with leaves and twigs. Nests are usually at least 10 feet above water.

Eggs: Female lays one clutch of 3–5 creamy-white eggs. Eggs are incubated for 27–32 days by both male and female.

Young: Eggs hatch about a month after being laid. Chicks will leave the nest after a day and fly within 8 weeks. Fledging takes place 2 months after hatching. They reach reproductive age around 4 years.

Predators: Raccoons, skunks, fish, snapping turtles, alligators, humans, snakes, and other wood storks

Migration: Mostly non-migrating, but juvenile birds have been observed moving north of nesting areas.

The wood stork is a large white bird with a bare head and neck of slate gray. Wings and tail are iridescent black to green. Feet, bill, and legs are black, and the toes are pink during breeding season. Immatures have a feather head and yellow-gray bill.

Did you know?

Alligator snapping turtles are the largest freshwater turtle species not only in Georgia, but also in North America! They can weigh over 200 pounds. Being that big, it has a bite force of 1,000 pounds. That's not the only amazing thing about their mouth; an alligator snapping turtle has a built-in "lure" (or skin protrusion) on its tongue that acts like bait to attract prey.

Most Active   Hibernates

Alligator Snapping Turtle

Macrochelys temminckii

Size: Male: 31 inches long; weighs 150–200 pounds.
Female: 20–22 inches long; weighs 60–63 pounds

Habitat: Rivers, streams, lakes, bayous, and swamps

Range: Alligator snapping turtles are endemic, or only found in the US. They can be found throughout Georgia.

Food: Carnivore who feeds on aquatic animals like fish, crawdads (crayfish), clams, mussels, and some plant materials, as well as birds and snakes

Mating: April to June and have to travel to find mates

Nest: Females will travel away from water sources on land and dig nest in sand or dirt.

Eggs: 1 clutch per year of around 10–60 spherical, whitish eggs with a leathery shell

Young: Eggs will hatch around 100 days after laying. Nest temperature determines sex at hatching: male turtles develop in cooler nest temperatures and females develop at warmer nest temperatures. They are fully independent at hatching, do not receive any care from parents, and reach sexual maturity around ages 11–16.

Predators: Raccoons, birds, otters, and fish will prey on eggs and juveniles. Adults are hunted by humans.

They have a spiked, dark-brown carapace. Alligator snapping turtles have 3 rows of raised scutes that resemble spikes on their carapace (back shell) that are brown to greenish gray. The plastron (bottom shell) is lighter than the carapace. They have a large triangular or spade-shaped head with a hooked beak.

Did you know?

The male alligator does not have vocal cords. The growling or roaring sound that males make in order to attract females comes from the alligator filling its lungs with air and exhaling. Alligators sometimes trick birds into landing or flying close to them by placing sticks and vegetation on their head; birds looking for nesting material will fly and try to retrieve the sticks and be met by the gator's mouth.

Most Active

American Alligator

Alligator mississippiensis

Size: 8–16 feet long; weighs up to 1,000 pounds

Habitat: Freshwater ponds, coastal areas, rivers, swamps, and brackish water (mix of fresh and saltwater)

Range: They are found throughout central and southern Georgia, as they are native to the southeastern US. Sometimes found in the Atlanta area

Food: Opportunistic carnivores that feed on snakes, fish, birds, mammals, insects, and sometimes even fruit

Mating: Starts in spring and goes until May or early June. Mating takes place at night. Males have multiple mates.

Nest: Nests are made of plant material and can be 3 feet tall by 7 feet wide. Eggs are covered with vegetation.

Eggs: 35–50 white eggs

Young: Eggs hatch about 2 months after laying. Hatchling sex is temperature dependent; nest temperatures below 88 degrees or above 90½ degrees are usually female, and temperatures of 89½ to around 90½ degrees are usually male. They reach independence at 1 year and reproductive age at around 10 years. Hatchlings form pods or groups and alert others to nearby danger by making clicking noises.

Predators: Humans; as juveniles: birds, snakes, bobcats, raccoons, otters, large fish, and older alligators

The American alligator is a thick-bodied reptile with short legs. It has a wide U-shaped snout. The body has thick skin that comes in colors of black to brownish gray; the tail is thick and muscular; the underside is white. Hatchlings are striped for the first several months. If the water freezes, alligators will bury themselves in mud and stick their snouts out for several days. **109**

Did you know?

Copperheads get their name from their copper- to bronze-colored head. A copperhead's size can give a hint to how large its fangs are. The larger or longer the snake, the longer the fangs usually are. Young copperheads are born with a bright-yellow tail that aids the young snake in catching prey. The snake moves its tail around like a worm to lure would-be food items.

Most Active   Hibernates

Copperhead

Agkistrodon contortrix

Size: 22–40 inches long; weighs 4–10 ounces or larger

Habitat: Dry rocky hillsides, lowland forest areas, grasslands, water-adjacent wooded areas, and suburban areas

Range: They live throughout the eastern and central US. They can be found statewide, except in southern Georgia.

Food: Carnivore. Adults eat mostly rodents like mice and rats but also baby cottontails, small birds, swamp rabbits, lizards, baby turtles, small snakes, amphibians, and insects (especially cicadas and grasshoppers).

Mating: April to May and late August to October. Males produce a pheromone that makes the female unattractive to other males.

Nest: Copperheads do not make nests but utilize natural dens or dens made from other animals. Dens are often near water sources, in rock crevices, hollowed-logs or downed trees, or in shrub piles.

Eggs: Copperheads are ovoviviparous: the eggs develop in the body, and the mother then gives live birth.

Young: Females give live birth to 5–8 (sometimes as many as 20) 6–10-inch-long young. These snakes reach sexual maturity at 4 years. They are independent at birth.

Predators: Snakes, raptors, raccoons, and opossums

Copperheads have a triangular or arrow-like, copper-bronze head. Eyes have vertical tear-shaped pupils. The thick body comes in varieties of tans, browns, dirty oranges, and copper. They have 10–18 hourglass-shaped bands. Copperheads are the only species with this hourglass shape. Juveniles have the same pattern but fewer hourglass shapes. They also have a yellow-tipped tail that fades away by age 3 or 4.

Did you know?
Cottonmouths are toxic but have a similar pattern to many different species of nonvenomous water snakes. One distinct feature that gives them away is the white lining of the mouth (hence the name cottonmouth), as well as the cream, white, or light-tan colors of the external (outside) portion of the mouth.

Most Active   Hibernates

Cottonmouth (Water Moccasin)

Agkistrodon piscivorus

Size: 2–4 feet long; weighs 2–4 pounds

Habitat: Forest, prairies, creeks, streams, marshes, swamps, coastal areas, and the shores of ponds and lakes

Range: Can be found in the eastern US. In Georgia, they are found almost statewide, except in northern Georgia and many counties that surround Atlanta.

Food: Birds, small turtles, fish, frogs, small mammals, snakes, lizards, and small alligators

Mating: April–May; males perform mating dances and fight over females.

Nest: No nest; they will use natural cavities in the ground or abandoned burrows of small mammals.

Eggs: No eggs are laid.

Young: These snakes are ovoviviparous, meaning the eggs develop in the body and then the mother gives live birth. Usually 5–9 live young are born, but as many as 16 can be born at one time. Snakelets are born 6 months after mating. At birth they are independent and receive no parental care.

Predators: Domestic cats, hawks, egrets, raccoons, eagles, large fish like longnose gars and largemouth bass, herons, and snapping turtles

Cottonmouth bodies come in various shades of dark colors from brown to black. The head is brown to tan with shades of yellowish browns. The bottom of the head is various shades of lighter hues of white, tan, brown, and cream colors with distinct facial markings. Cottonmouths have a series of 10 or more bands across their back. Their eyes are like those of cats, with vertical pupils.

Did you know?

Terrapins are the only turtles in the world that live in brackish water (mix of salt and freshwater). They have special glands called lachrymal salt glands that help them get rid of salt in the body. Terrapins have powerful jaws that help them in eating different types of animals with shells, like snails and clams. Diamondback terrapins get their name from the diamond-shaped markings on their carapace (top shell).

Most Active   Hibernates

Diamondback Terrapin

Malaclemys terrapin

Size: Male: 5½–6 inches long; weighs ½ pound.
Female: 11–12 inches long; weighs 1½ pounds

Habitat: Coastal areas like estuaries, tidal creeks, salt marshes, mangroves, and lagoons

Range: They can be found as far north as Massachusetts and as far south as the Florida Keys, and westward into Texas. In Georgia, they are found along the 100 miles of natural coastline in tidal marshes.

Food: Fish, crabs, mussels, marine snails, insects, carrion (dead things), clams, and other mollusks

Mating: May–June

Nest: Nests are usually in sand dunes or scrub vegetation.

Eggs: Female will lay 2 or 3 clutches a year. Clutches range from 4–23 eggs, but usually 5–10 pinkish-white eggs.

Young: Hatchlings usually emerge 2–3 months after laying and are fully independent at hatching. Like other turtles, terrapins have temperature-dependent sex determination. Females mature around year 7, but due to their smaller size, males mature around 2 or 3 years.

Predators: Wild hogs, herons, raccoons, humans, crabs, rats, gulls, crows, minks, and foxes

The diamondback terrapin is a species of turtle native to the eastern and southern United States and Bermuda. The shell appears wedge-shaped and can vary from brown to gray. The body can be gray, brown, yellow, or white. All have a unique pattern of wiggly, black markings or spots on their body and head. Diamondback terrapins have large, webbed feet and are very strong swimmers.

Did you know?

The eastern coral snake is venomous, even though it does not have an arrow-shaped head. This proves that what's true for some venomous snakes is not true for all venomous snakes. Western coral snakes are the only snakes in the eastern part of the US that have fangs fixed in the front of their mouth.

Most Active   Hibernates

Eastern Coral Snake

Micrurus fulvius

Size: 18–30 inches long (rarely over 17 inches); weight ranges widely

Habitat: Grasslands, suburban areas, flatwoods and scrub areas, woodlands, forests, wetlands and the borders of swamps, and coastal plain areas like sandhills

Range: Eastern coral snakes can be found from the southeastern parts of North Carolina through Florida and the southern parts of Georgia, as well as Alabama and Mississippi into the southeastern areas of Louisiana.

Food: Frogs, snakes, lizards, insects, and sometimes mammals

Mating: Late spring to early fall

Nest: No nest; they will use natural cavities in the ground or abandoned burrows of small mammals. The eggs are often laid underground or in leaf litter.

Eggs: 4–12 white, leathery eggs that are elongated

Young: Snakelets hatch around 2 months after laying. They are around 7–9 inches at hatching. No parental care is given. Females become mature around 21 months and males become mature around 11–21 months.

Predators: Snakes, raptors like American kestrels and hawks, bullfrogs, loggerhead shrikes, and cats. Eggs and juveniles are vulnerable to red ants.

Eastern coral snakes have a striped body with a pattern of red, black, and yellow bands or rings. The red and yellow touch, followed by the black. The nose is black with the rest of the head being yellow. The red stripes have black specks within them. Juveniles have a similar pattern as the adults but brighter in color. The pattern darkens as the snake ages.

Did you know?

Eastern garter snakes are highly social and will form groups with other snakes and often other species to overwinter together in a burrow or hole. When threatened by a predator or handled, they will sometimes musk or emit a foul-smelling, oily substance from their cloaca (butt).

Most Active   Hibernates

Eastern Garter Snake

Thamnophis sirtalis

Size: 14–36 inches long (rarely over 17 inches); weighs 5–5½ ounces

Habitat: Forests and forest edges, grasslands, and suburban areas

Range: They are found throughout Georgia and can be found in the eastern US from Minnesota, southward to eastern Texas, and then east towards the Atlantic coast.

Food: Frogs, snails, toads, salamanders, insects, fish, and worms

Mating: April or May

Nest: No nest; they will use natural cavities in the ground or abandoned burrows of small mammals.

Eggs: No eggs are laid. Eastern garter snakes are born live in a litter of between 8 and 20 snakes.

Young: Snakelets are 4½–9 inches long at birth; no parental care is given.

Predators: Crows, ravens, hawks, owls, raccoons, foxes, and squirrels

Eastern garter snakes are black with three yellow stripes running down their body on the back and sides. They withstand winter by gathering in groups inside the burrows of rodents or under human-made structures, and they enter brumation, or a state of slowed body activity.

Did you know?

The eastern glass lizard is not a snake, though it lacks legs like snakes. A few characteristics that let us know that it is a lizard is that it has eyelids that move (snakes do not have eyelids) and its tail is as long, or longer, than its body. Eastern glass lizards get their name from how their tails detach when they are scared or captured. The detached tail separates from the body, making it look like the lizard has shattered into pieces.

Most Active   Hibernates

Eastern Glass Lizard

Ophisaurus ventralis

Size: 18–42½ inches long; weighs 11–21 ounces

Habitat: Coastal plains, forests, savannas, shrubland wetlands, wet meadows, maritime forests, grasslands, damp grassy areas, and sandy environments such as dunes

Range: Their range spans from southern Florida up through Georgia into North Carolina and as far west as Louisiana. In Georgia, their range extends from the central portion to the south.

Food: Carnivores that feed on a variety of prey such as small mice, grasshoppers, spiders, snails, beetles, and the eggs of reptiles and birds

Mating: Late spring through the end of summer

Nest: Nests are usually depressions in sandy soil or under natural covering. The female will guard the eggs until they hatch.

Eggs: 5–15 eggs are laid in June and July.

Young: Young are born in August and September. They are 7 inches long, khaki to beige, with dark stripes along the side. The young are independent at hatching.

Predators: Hawks, raccoons, foxes, coyotes, bobcats, skunks, and other mammals. Several snake species also feed on glass lizards.

Eastern glass lizards are black with greenish-yellow-to-tan markings trailing down their body from their nose down to their tail. The nose and underside are various shades of tans and yellows. Juveniles are khaki or beige to brown in color overall with black streak markings going down both sides.

Did you know?

The eastern indigo snake is the longest native snake species that is found in North America. Eastern indigo snakes get their name from the iridescence that they have on their scales. In the right light, the color looks deep blue or purplish.

Most Active   Hibernates

Eastern Indigo Snake

Drymarchon couperi

Size: 5–7 feet long; weighs 6–10 pounds

Habitat: Sandhill habitats, shady creek bottoms, flatwoods, stream bottoms, cane fields, forests, wetlands, shrublands, prairies, pine forests, coastal dunes, and areas with gopher tortoises

Range: Eastern indigo snakes range from extreme southwestern South Carolina south through Florida and west to southern Alabama and southeastern Mississippi. In Georgia they are found in the southeastern corner of the state, as well as in areas that border Florida and southeastern Alabama.

Food: Carnivore that feeds on turtles, toads, lizards, eggs, frogs, mammals, snakes, and birds

Mating: November–April

Nest: Abandoned burrows or fallen logs

Eggs: 6–12 eggs per clutch

Young: Snakelets hatch after around 3 months. They are between 16 inches and 2 feet long and are completely independent when hatched. They reach maturity around year 3 or 4.

Predators: Alligators, snakes, domesticated dogs and cats, red-tailed hawks, humans

The eastern indigo snake has a brick-red-to-orange throat and cheeks; their underside is a charcoal-blackish gray. Immature indigos are a glossy black with white-and-hazy-blue bands down their body.

Did you know?

Kingsnakes get their name because they eat a variety of different snake species, many of which are venomous. It's a good thing kingsnakes have a resistance to venom. Eastern kingsnakes will mimic rattlesnakes when disturbed, vibrating their tails.

Most Active   Hibernates

Eastern Kingsnake

Lampropeltis getula

Size: 36–48 inches long; weighs 4–5 pounds

Habitat: Hardwood forests, swamps, pine forest, fields, fresh-water marshes, and city areas

Range: Southern New Jersey to Northern Florida, west to the Appalachians

Food: Rodents, birds, snakes, lizards, and turtle eggs

Mating: March–May

Nest: Nests are usually in abandoned burrows, under a log, or made in moist soil.

Eggs: 4–20 white eggs

Young: Hatchlings emerge 60 days after eggs are laid; the young are brightly colored and weighing around 9–14 grams and approximately 5–8 inches long. Females become reproductively mature around 2–3 years and males around 1–2 years.

Predators: Raccoons, snakes, hawks, alligators, skunks, and opossums

The eastern kingsnake is a thick black snake with small eyes. Scales are smooth. It has white-to-yellow bands across the back. Snakes from mountainous areas usually have thinner bands or are almost completely black, and snakes from the coastal plain have wider bands.

Did you know?

The eastern tiger salamander can grow up to 13 inches long and live over 20 years! Eastern tiger salamanders migrate to their birthplace in order to breed, sometimes over a mile or more. Eastern tiger salamanders have a hidden weapon! They produce a poisonous toxin that is secreted or released from two glands in their tail. This toxin makes them taste bad to predators and allows them to escape.

Most Active   Hibernates

Eastern Tiger Salamander

Ambystoma tigrinum

Size: 7–13 inches long; weighs 4½ ounces

Habitat: Woodlands, marshes, and meadows; they spend most of their time underground in burrows.

Range: They are found across much of the state; populations are also found in the western United States.

Food: Carnivores (eat meat); insects, frogs, worms, and snails

Mating: Tiger salamanders leave their burrows to find standing bodies of fresh water. They breed in late winter and early spring after the ground has thawed.

Nest: No nest, but eggs are joined together into one group in a jelly-like sack called an egg mass. An egg mass is attached to grass, leaves, and other plant material at the bottom of a pond.

Eggs: There are 20–100 eggs or more in an egg mass.

Young: Eggs hatch after 2 weeks, and the young are fully aquatic with external gills. Limbs develop shortly after hatching; within 3 months, the young are fully grown but will hang around in a vernal pool. Individuals living in permanent ponds can take up to 6 months to fully develop.

Predators: Young are preyed upon by diving beetles, fish, turtles, and herons. Adults are preyed upon by snakes, owls, and badgers.

Eastern tiger salamanders have thick black, brown, or grayish bodies with uneven spots of yellow, tan, brown, or green along the head and body. The underside is usually a variation of yellow. Males are usually larger and thicker than females.

Did You Know?

Gopher tortoises are keystone species, meaning that other animals depend on them for their survival. Over 350 species of animals depend on or benefit from the burrows that Gopher tortoises make. These burrows are on average 15 feet long and over 6 feet deep. Some tortoises make burrows that are over 30 feet long and 10 feet deep. The gopher tortoise is the only native species of tortoises that can be found east of the Mississippi River.

Most Active   Hibernates

Gopher Tortoise

Gopherus polyphemus

Size: 9–15 inches long; weighs 10–13 pounds

Habitat: Longleaf pine sandhills, scrub, pine flatwoods, coastal grasslands, dunes, and prairies

Range: Gopher tortoises can be found in the coastal plain area of the United States from the most southern areas of South Carolina, south through Georgia and Florida, and westward to eastern Louisiana. In Georgia, they can be found from the south-central part of the state southward into Florida.

Food: Herbivores (plant eaters) that feed on grasses, fruits, and flowers. Sometimes they will eat carrion (dead things).

Mating: March–October

Nest: Usually occurs in areas that are bare and receive a lot of sun. Oftentimes there is a mounded area in front of the burrow, also known as the burrow apron.

Eggs: 5–9 white, sphere-shaped, Ping-Pong-ball-size eggs

Young: Hatchlings emerge about 2 inches long 90–110 days after laying. They are independent at the time of hatching. Males reach adulthood in around 9–12 years and females around 10–21 years.

Predators: Eagles, raccoons, bears, hawks, foxes, coyotes, bobcats, armadillos, fire ants, skunks, and dogs

Gopher tortoises have a smushed dome-shaped carapace that is somewhat flattened and comes in shades of brown and gray. Skin is scaly and can be shades of gray to tan and brown. They have forelimbs that are flat and aid in digging. Juveniles have yellow-hued skin and scutes (hard plates on the shell) that are yellow in the center and get darker with age.

129

Did you know?

The green anole is the only species of anole that is native to the United States. The male does pushups to attract a mate and defend its territory. They will extend the dewlap (a skin fold under the chin) and bob their head up and down in the presence of a rival male. Green anoles can change colors! Although not as elaborate as chameleons, they can change to various shades of green and brown.

Most Active

Green Anole

Anolis carolinensis

Size: 5–8 inches long; weighs 1-6 grams, the same as a penny or two

Habitat: Moist forests, coastal areas, shrublands, urban areas, swamps, and farmlands

Range: Anoles are found throughout the southeastern US. In Georgia, they are statewide, except in areas of the Blue Ridge Mountains.

Food: Carnivore that feeds on insects and other soft-bodied animals like spiders, flies, crickets, and grasshoppers.

Mating: April–September, males will patrol a territory and defend it from other males. Males attract females by extending their dewlap (pink-colored skin under chin) and bobbing up and down.

Nest: Shallow depression in soft soil, leaf litter, compost, rotting wood, or even a hole in a nearby tree

Eggs: 1–10 soft-shelled eggs are laid 2 to 4 weeks after mating.

Young: Hatching takes place 30–45 days after laying. Anoles are 2–2½ inches at hatching and are fully independent.

Predators: Lizards, birds, cats, dogs, frogs, and snakes

Green anoles come in many shades of greens and browns. What color you see depends on their surroundings and the condition that they are in. Males have a bright-red-to-ruby-pink skinfold or dewlap that extends under the chin. This dewlap serves a dual purpose of finding mates and deterring rival males from entering its territory. The female dewlap is much smaller and comes in shades of pink to almost white. Females have a white stripe that runs along their back.

Did you know?

Loggerhead turtles get their odd name because sailors originally mistook them for logs or tree trunks. Unlike other sea turtles, green sea turtles are mostly herbivores (plant eaters). They eat algae and other plants, which gives their fat and muscles a greenish tint, leading to their name!

Most Active

Loggerhead Sea Turtle (LST)/
Green Sea Turtle (GST)

Caretta caretta / Chelonia mydas

Size: LST: 2½–3½ feet long; weighs 200–375 pounds.
GST: 3–4½ feet long; weighs 250–500 pounds

Habitat: Coastal areas and open ocean

Range: LST: Found on the Florida coast, especially in summer. GST: Found around the world where the water is warm enough.

Food: LST: Crabs, jellyfish, conches, fish. GST: Seagrass and algae

Mating: (LST) May–August and (GST) June–September. Mating takes place every 2–4 years.

Nest: LST: A cavity around 18 inches deep. GST: A cavity about 30 inches deep. Both species nest above the surf line (where waves crash) on beaches. Females can lay multiple batches of eggs a season and usually will lay a new nest after about 14 days or so.

Eggs: LST: 100-130 eggs; GST: 100-130 eggs. Ping-Pong-ball size

Young: After 2 months of incubating, hatchlings emerge and immediately travel toward the ocean.

Predators: Feral hogs, sharks, raccoons, dogs, humans, crows, birds, fish, ants, crabs, cats, coyotes, foxes, bears, and skunks

Loggerheads have a distinctive large head and heart-shaped carapace (shell) that ranges from brown to red. The underside is paler and yellow to off-white. Green sea turtles are the second-largest sea turtle (the leatherback is bigger). Their shell is dark brown to olive colored with a yellow-to-pale plastron (underside).

Did you know?

When threatened, a rattlesnake shakes its rattle to warn would-be predators. These snakes are all venomous (their bites inject venom, a toxin), so do not go near one or try to pick one up! Instead, leave it alone, so it can help people by munching on rodents and other pests! Rattlesnakes are "pit vipers," snakes that have a special body part that helps them "see" heat.

Most Active   Hibernates

Rattlesnakes

Eastern Diamondback Rattlesnake (EDR) (*Crotalus adamanteus*), Timber Rattlesnake (TR) (*Crotalus horridus*), Pygmy Rattlesnake (PR) (*Sistrurus miliarius*)

Size: EDR: 33–72 inches long; weighs 10 pounds. TR: 36–40 inches long; weighs 1–2 pounds. PR: 14–22 inches long; weighs 5½ ounces

Habitat: EDR: Elevated areas near floodplains and swamps, forests, dunes; TR: Lowland forests near water; PR: Scrublands, coastal areas, forests, swamps

Range: EDR: Southern Georgia and the southeastern US; TR: Most of Georgia, found across much of the eastern US; PR: Most of Georgia, except the northern border

Food: EDR: Small mammals, birds. TR: Rabbits, squirrels, rats, mice, birds, other snakes, lizards, and frogs. PR: Insects, small mammals, frogs, and lizards

Mating: September–January; mating occurs in the summer and fall. Males display a courtship "dance."

Nest: The mother gives birth in a burrow or hollow log.

Eggs: They are ovoviviparous, which means the eggs hatch inside of the female and snakes are born live.

Young: EDR: 6–21 snakelets are born; around 15 inches long. TR: Females give birth to 12 or more young; around 10–18 inches long. PR: Give birth to 1–12 young

Predators: Coyotes, humans, bobcats, skunks, foxes, hawks, and owls; kingsnakes, indigo snakes, and cottonmouths

Eastern diamondback: Brown, yellow, or tan, with black, gray, or brownish diamond. Timber: Gray, brown, or pink, with brown or orange stripes. Pygmy: Gray to black with hints of orange, and brown lines down the back. All have catlike pupils.

Did you know?

The snapping turtle's sex is determined by the temperature of the nest! Nest temperatures that are 67–68 degrees produce females, temperatures in the range between 70 and 72 degrees produce both males and females, and nests that are 73–75 degrees will usually produce all males.

Most Active

Snapping Turtle, Common

Chelydra serpentina

Size: 8–16 inches long; weighs 10–35 pounds

Habitat: Rivers, marshes, and lakes; can be found in areas that have brackish water (freshwater and saltwater mixture)

Range: They are found throughout Georgia; also found in the eastern US and southern Canada.

Food: These omnivores (eat both plants and animals) eat frogs, reptiles, snakes, birds, small mammals, and plants.

Mating: April to November are the breeding months; lays eggs during June and July

Nest: Females dig a hole in sandy soil and lay the eggs into it.

Eggs: 25–42 eggs, sometimes as many as 80 or more

Young: Like sea turtles, snapping turtles have temperature-dependent sex determination (TSD), meaning the temperature of the nest determines the sex of the young. Hatchlings leave the nest between August and October. In the North, turtles mature at around 15–20 years, while southern turtles mature around 12 years old.

Predators: Raccoons, skunks, crows, dogs, and humans

The snapping turtle's carapace (top shell) is dark green to brown and usually covered in algae or moss. The plastron (or bottom of the shell) is smaller than the carapace. They are crepuscular animals that are mostly active during the dawn and dusk hours. Young turtles will actively look for food. As adults, they rely heavily on ambushing to hunt; they bury themselves in the sand with just the tip of their nose and eyes showing.

Glossary

Adaptation—An animal's physical (outward) or behavioral (inward) adjustment to changes in the environment.

Amphibian—A small animal with a backbone, has moist skin, and lacks scales. Most amphibians start out as an egg, live at least part of their life in water, and finish life as a land dweller.

Biome—A part or region of Earth that has a particular type of climate and animals and plants that adapted to live in the area.

Bird—A group of animals that all have two legs and feet, a beak, feathers, and wings; while not all birds fly, all birds lay eggs.

Brood—A group of young birds that hatch at the same time and with the same mother.

Carnivore—An animal that primarily eats other animals.

Clutch—The number of eggs an animal lays during one nesting period; an animal can lay more than one clutch each season.

Crepuscular—The hours before sunset or just after sunrise; some animals have adapted to be most active during these low-light times.

Diurnal—During the day; many animals are most active during the daytime.

Ecosystem—A group of animals and plants that interact with each other and the physical area that they live in.

Evolution—A process of change in a species or a group of animals that are all the same kind; evolution happens over several generations or in a group of animals living around the same time; evolution happens through adaptation, or physical and biological changes to better fit the environment over time.

Fledgling—A baby bird that has developed flight feathers and has left the nest.

Gestation—The length of time a developing animal is carried in its mother's womb.

Herbivore—An animal that primarily eats plants.

Hibernate—A survival strategy or process where animals "slow down" and go into a long period of reduced activity to survive winter or seasonal changes; during hibernation, activities like feeding, breathing, and converting food to energy all stop.

Incubate—When a bird warms eggs by sitting on them.

Invasive—A nonnative animal that outcompetes native animals in a particular area, harming the environment.

Mammal—An air-breathing, warm-blooded, fur- or hair-covered animal with a backbone. All mammals produce milk and usually give birth to live young.

Migration—When animals move from one area to another. Migration usually occurs seasonally, but it can also happen due to biological processes, such as breeding.

Molt—When animals shed or drop their skin, feathers, or shell.

Nocturnal—At night; many animals are most active at night.

Nonnative—An organism introduced (by humans) into a new area.

Omnivore—An animal that eats both plants and other animals.

Predator—An animal that hunts (and eats) other animals.

Raptor—A group of birds that all have a curved beak and sharp talons, which hunt or feed on other animals. Also known as a bird of prey.

Reptile—An egg-laying, air-breathing, cold-blooded animal that has a backbone and skin made of scales, which crawls on its belly or uses stubby legs to get around.

Scat—The waste product that animals release from their bodies; another word for it is poop or droppings.

Talon—The claw on the feet see on raptors and birds of prey.

Torpor—A form of hibernation in which an animal slows down its breathing, and heart rate; torpor ranges from a few hours at a time to a whole day; torpor does not involve a deep sleep.

Checklist

Mammals

- ☐ American Beaver
- ☐ Big Brown Bat
- ☐ Black Bear
- ☐ Bobcat
- ☐ Coyote
- ☐ Eastern Chipmunk
- ☐ Eastern Cottontail
- ☐ Eastern Fox Squirrel
- ☐ Gray Fox
- ☐ Long-tailed Weasel
- ☐ Manatee (West Indian Manatee)
- ☐ Mink
- ☐ Northern Raccoon
- ☐ Northern River Otter
- ☐ Red Fox
- ☐ Southeastern Pocket Gopher
- ☐ Southern Flying Squirrel
- ☐ Spotted Skunk
- ☐ Star-nosed Mole
- ☐ Tricolored Bat
- ☐ Virginia Opossum
- ☐ White-tailed Deer

Birds

- ☐ American Goldfinch
- ☐ Anhinga
- ☐ Bald Eagle
- ☐ Barred Owl
- ☐ Belted Kingfisher
- ☐ Black Vulture/ Turkey Vulture
- ☐ Canada Goose
- ☐ Double-crested Cormorant
- ☐ Eastern Towhee
- ☐ Gray Catbird
- ☐ Great Blue Heron
- ☐ Great Horned Owl
- ☐ Mallard
- ☐ Northern Cardinal
- ☐ Northern Mockingbird
- ☐ Osprey
- ☐ Painted Bunting
- ☐ Peregrine Falcon
- ☐ Red-tailed Hawk/ Red-shouldered Hawk
- ☐ Roseate Spoonbill
- ☐ Ruby-throated Hummingbird

- ☐ White Ibis
- ☐ Wild Turkey
- ☐ Wood Duck
- ☐ Wood Stork

Reptiles and Amphibians

- ☐ Alligator Snapping Turtle
- ☐ American Alligator
- ☐ Copperhead
- ☐ Cottonmouth (Water Moccasin)
- ☐ Diamondback Terrapin
- ☐ Eastern Coral Snake
- ☐ Eastern Garter Snake
- ☐ Eastern Glass Lizard
- ☐ Eastern Indigo Snake
- ☐ Eastern Kingsnake
- ☐ Eastern Tiger Salamander
- ☐ Gopher Tortoise
- ☐ Green Anole
- ☐ Loggerhead Sea Turtle/ Green Sea Turtle
- ☐ Rattlesnakes
- ☐ Snapping Turtle, Common

The Art of Conservation®

Featuring two signature programs, The Songbird Art Contest™ and The Fish Art Contest®, the Art of Conservation programs celebrate the arts as a cornerstone to conservation. To enter, youth artists create an original hand-drawn illustration and written essay, story, or poem synthesizing what they have learned. The contests are FREE to enter and open to students in K-12. For program updates, rules, guidelines, and entry forms, visit: www.TheArtofConservation.org

The Fish Art Contest® introduces youth to the wonders of fish, the joy of fishing, and the importance of aquatic conservation.
The Fish Art Contest uses art, science, and creative writing to foster connections to the outdoors and inspire the next generation of stewards. Participants are encouraged to use the Fish On! lesson plan, then submit an original, handmade piece of artwork to compete for prizes and international recognition.

The Songbird Art Contest® explores the wonders and species diversity of North American songbirds. Raising awareness and educating the public on bird conservation, the Songbird program builds stewardship, encourages outdoors participation, and promotes the discovery of nature.

Photo Credits

About the Author

Alex Troutman is a wildlife biologist, birder, nature enthusiast, and science communicator from Austell, Georgia. He has a passion for sharing the wonders of nature and introducing the younger generation to the outdoors. He holds both a bachelor's degree and a master's degree in biology from Georgia Southern University (the Real GSU), with a focus in conservation. Because he knows what it feels like to not see individuals who look like you, or come from a similar background, doing

the things you enjoy or working in the career that you aspire to be in, Alex makes a point not only to be that representation for the younger generation, but also to make sure that kids have exposure to the careers they are interested in and the diverse scientists working in those careers.

Alex is the co-organizer of several Black in X weeks, including Black Birders Week, Black Mammologists Week, and Black in Marine Science Week. This movement encourages diversity in nature, the celebration of Black individual scientists, awareness of Black nature enthusiasts, and diversity in STEAM fields.